NEW WORDS TO OLD TUNES

New Words to Old Tunes

Genres and Metrics of Lebanese Zajal Poetry

Adnan Haydar

UNIVERSITY OF CAMBRIDGE
Faculty of Asian and Middle Eastern Studies

OpenBook Publishers

https://www.openbookpublishers.com

All external links were active at the time of publication unless otherwise stated and have been archived via the Internet Archive Wayback Machine at https://archive.org/web

Any digital material and resources associated with this volume will be available at https://doi.org/10.11647/OBP.0424#resources

Semitic Languages and Cultures 33

ISSN (print): 2632-6906
ISSN (digital): 2632-6914

ISBN Paperback: 978-1-80511-391-1
ISBN Hardback: 978-1-80511-392-8
ISBN Digital (PDF): 978-1-80511-393-5

DOI: 10.11647/OBP.0424

Cover image: Moustafa Farroukh, A View from Keserwan (ca. 1938), https://commons.wikimedia.org/wiki/File:A_View_from_Keserwan.png.
Cover design: Jeevanjot Kaur Nagpal

The fonts used in this volume are Charis SIL and Scheherazade New.

Cambridge Semitic Languages and Cultures

General Editor: Geoffrey Khan

This is the first Open Access book series in the field; it combines the high peer-review and editorial standards with the fair Open Access model offered by OBP. The series includes philological and linguistic studies of Semitic languages, editions of Semitic texts, and studies of Semitic cultures. Titles cover all periods, traditions and methodological approaches to the field. The editorial board comprises Geoffrey Khan, Aaron Hornkohl, Esther-Miriam Wagner, Anne Burberry, and Benjamin Kantor.

You can access the full series catalogue here: https://www.openbookpublishers.com/series/2632-6914

If you would like to join our community and interact with authors of the books, sign up to be contacted about events relating to the series and receive publication updates and news here: https://forms.gle/RWymsw3hdsUjZTXv5

For Paula

TABLE OF CONTENTS

Acknowledgements ix

List of Audio Recordings xiii

List of Figures xvii

Introduction 1

1. Terms and Methodology 9

2. Previous Scholarship on *Zajal* Metrics 25

3. *Fuṣḥā* and *Zajal* Metres 63

4. The Role of Stress in the Scansion of *Zajal* Genres 73

5. *Qarrādī* and Its Various Manifestations 103

6. *ʿAtābā, Mījanā,* and Other Popular Genres 129

Conclusion 193

References 197

Index 201

ACKNOWLEDGEMENTS

This work could not have come to fruition without the support and guidance of many individuals and institutions. Over the course of thirty years, countless colleagues, *zajal* enthusiasts, friends, and family members have accompanied this manuscript's journey.

First and foremost, my deepest gratitude goes to my wife, Paula, whose unwavering support has been a cornerstone of this project. She embraced every word and dedicated countless hours to navigating the complexities of the text: handling transliterations, musical notations, poetic scansion symbols, audio files, and other technical challenges. Her persistent encouragement kept me moving forward.

I remain forever indebted to the late Dr Lois al-Faruqi, who spent numerous hours with me in my office at the University of Pennsylvania. Her meticulous transcription of musical notations and her deep knowledge of Arabic music were indispensable to this study.

The foundation for this project was laid by the late Dr Mansour Ajami, who graciously sang various *zajal* genres for me in his home near Princeton University. His recordings served as the basis for my entire analysis.

I would also like to express my heartfelt thanks to the late Professor Israel Katz, ethnomusicologist at Columbia University. His generous invitation to his home and his careful analysis of choral renditions helped to extract the proto-tune for *maʿannā* and *qarrādī*, two central genres of *zajal* poetry.

My thanks go as well to Dr Manny Rubin, Professor of Music at the University of Massachusetts Amherst, whose passion for Fayrouz's *Mkhammas mardūd* made the transcription of its musical notations a labour of love.

I owe special recognition to Clayton Clark, my graduate assistant at the University of Arkansas, whose expertise transformed my manuscript and its accompanying cassette recordings into digital form.

I am deeply grateful to Dr Youssef Tannous, Dean of the Faculty of Music at Holy Spirit University of Kaslik (Lebanon), for his invaluable feedback on the manuscript and for overseeing his team's review of the musical notations. Special thanks to Dr Henri Zoghaib, whose introductions and countless conversations on the Lebanese *zajal* tradition have enriched my work.

My profound gratitude also goes to poet, writer, and artist Joseph Abi Daher, whose extensive writings on Lebanese vernacular poetry have greatly informed my understanding of *zajal*.

To the many talented *zajal* poets I've had the honour of consulting throughout my life, I offer my deepest thanks. In particular, I would like to acknowledge the late Zaghlūl al-Dāmūr (Joseph al-Hāshim), whose interviews were filled with generous insights into his art. I am equally grateful to my dear friends, poets Antoine Saadeh and Elias Khalil, who continue to inspire my love of Lebanese *zajal* and draw me back to Lebanon each summer to witness their performances.

I am also indebted to the University of Pennsylvania, the University of Massachusetts Amherst, and the University of

Arkansas for providing the resources and motivation to pursue this research.

I would like to express my sincere gratitude to those at Cambridge Semitic Languages and Cultures Series, whose careful review and editorial support were crucial to shaping this book.

Finally, I offer my heartfelt thanks to my parents, Yolanda and Fuad; my brother, Nabil; and my children, Tarik, Samir, Nadia, and Fuad, for their patience and encouragement throughout this long journey.

LIST OF AUDIO RECORDINGS

The Role of Stress in the Scansion of *Zajal* Genres

Recording 1: *Maʿannā* #1 (41s)
https://hdl.handle.net/20.500.12434/352fd301

Recording 2: *Maʿannā* #2 (47s)
https://hdl.handle.net/20.500.12434/0267921a

Recording 3: *Qarrādī* #1 (27s)
https://hdl.handle.net/20.500.12434/cf56cbf4

Recording 4: *Qarrādī* #2 (30s)
https://hdl.handle.net/20.500.12434/d2c44fef

Recording 5: *Qarrādī* #3 (19s)
https://hdl.handle.net/20.500.12434/359dcb61

Qarrādī and Its Various Manifestations

Recording 6: *Afrāmiyya* (1m 19s)
https://hdl.handle.net/20.500.12434/e18e7d75

Recording 7: *Layyā w-layyā* (17s)
https://hdl.handle.net/20.500.12434/b4a6b4ea

Recording 8: *ʿAl-yādī* (26s)
https://hdl.handle.net/20.500.12434/ae9b02ae

Recording 9: *Ya-ghzayyil* (43s)
https://hdl.handle.net/20.500.12434/86c6f703

Recording 10: *Huzām* (47s)
https://hdl.handle.net/20.500.12434/29ac227a

Recording 11: *Biqāʿī* (34s)
https://hdl.handle.net/20.500.12434/135ea560

Recording 12: *Bayrūtī* (36s)
https://hdl.handle.net/20.500.12434/bb37e5cd

ʿAtābā, Mījanā, and Popular Genres

Recording 13: *Mījanā* (22s)
https://hdl.handle.net/20.500.12434/b4508329

Recording 14: *ʿAtābā* (1m 22s)
https://hdl.handle.net/20.500.12434/edce4ce1

Recording 15: Short *qaṣīd* (9s)
https://hdl.handle.net/20.500.12434/53b3aa1a

Recording 16: Middle *qaṣīd* (11s)
https://hdl.handle.net/20.500.12434/0bb108db

Recording 17: Long *qaṣīd* (11s)
https://hdl.handle.net/20.500.12434/2f2f70df

Recording 18: *Ḥidā* (34s)
https://hdl.handle.net/20.500.12434/56dc3134

Recording 19: *Nadb* (20s)
https://hdl.handle.net/20.500.12434/8e1e009d

Recording 20: *Nadb* #1 (25s)
https://hdl.handle.net/20.500.12434/e501be1a

Recording 21: *Nadb* #2 (18s)
https://hdl.handle.net/20.500.12434/011231ce

Recording 22: *Nadb* #3 (27s)
https://hdl.handle.net/20.500.12434/7b8abb9b

Recording 23: *Ḥawraba* (20s)
https://hdl.handle.net/20.500.12434/c6a4fb43

Recording 24: *Zalghaṭa* (17s)
https://hdl.handle.net/20.500.12434/a07a4f76

Recording 25: *Abū al-zuluf* (1m 33s)
https://hdl.handle.net/20.500.12434/18f75833

Recording 26: *Shurūqī* (1m 17s)
https://hdl.handle.net/20.500.12434/18436656

Recording 27: *Mawwāl baghdādī* (2m 49s)
https://hdl.handle.net/20.500.12434/8dde3b55

Recording 28: *Mkhammas mardūd* (2m 30s)
https://hdl.handle.net/20.500.12434/a172c611

Recordings 1–27 were made by the author from 1975 to 1977 in Princeton, New Jersey, and in 2023 in Fayetteville, Arkansas. Recordings 1–27 are sung by Dr Mansour Ajami, except for recordings 15, 16, 17, and 24 which are sung by the author. Recording 28 is sung by Fayrouz.

LIST OF FIGURES

The Role of Stress in the Scansion of *Zajal* Genres

Figure 1: *Maʿannā* #1

Figure 2: *Maʿannā* #2

Figure 3: *Qarrādī* #1

Figure 4: *Qarrādī* #2

Figure 5: *Qarrādī* #3

Figure 6: Proto-tune

Figure 7: Line 6 of *maʿannā* #1

***Qarrādī* and Its Various Manifestations**

Figure 8: The three tunes

Figure 9: *Huzām/khuzām*

Figure 10: *Biqāʿī*

Figure 11: *Bayrūtī*

ʿ*Atābā*, *Mījanā*, and Popular Genres

Figure 12: *Mījanā* refrain #1

Figure 13: *Mījanā* refrain #2

Figure 14: *ʿAtābā*

Figure 15: The short *qaṣīd*

Figure 16: The middle *qaṣīd*

Figure 17: The long *qaṣīd*

Figure 18: Superimposition of musical rhythm and accents with poetic meter, illustrating the alignment between rhythmic beats and metrical stresses

Figure 19: *Ḥidā*
Figure 20: *Nadb*
Figure 21: *Nadb* #1
Figure 22: *Nadb* #2
Figure 23: *Nadb* #3
Figure 24: *Ḥawraba*
Figure 25: *Zalghaṭa*
Figure 26: *Abū al-zuluf*
Figure 27: *Shurūqī*
Figure 28: Proto-tune
Figure 29: *Al-mawwāl al-baghdādī*
Figure 30: *Mkhammas mardūd*

On figures 1–29, musical notations were transcribed from the audio recordings of Dr Mansour Ajami by the late musicologist Lois al-Faruqi in 1977 and photographed by the author. The musical notation on Figure 30 was transcribed by Professor Israel Katz in 1978 and photographed by the author.

INTRODUCTION

"*Zajal* is to Lebanon what the Pyramids are to Egypt, the Louvre is to France, and the Taj Mahal to India"

Saʿīd ʿAql

It was on a hot day in the summer of 1958 when all the walls and telephone poles in my small village in Lebanon were plastered with announcements about a *zajal* encounter that was to take place in a neighbouring village. I was seventeen years old then, and I had already attended one *zajal* event in my own village. That memorable and exciting event left an indelible mark on me, and since then I became an aficionado of *zajal* and tried to take advantage of as many of the performances staged in the neighbouring villages as I could.

Typically, *zajal* performances are staged in a sports arena or any space that can accommodate a thousand or more spectators. A stage is set up facing the audience. Two tables are placed on the stage, surrounded by four chairs each. There are empty glasses that are about to be filled with arak, the popular Lebanese alcoholic drink, and an array of small plates with traditional Lebanese mezze (hors d'oeuvres).

As the arena starts filling up with *zajal* enthusiasts, eight poets, four from each *jawqa* ('troupe'), take their places at the two tables. Behind them sits a chorus group, called the *riddādeh* ('repeaters'). Their job is to sing the poets' ending couplets as a musical refrain and to help keep the poets in tune. A few minutes later, one of the poets raises and shakes his tambourine,

https://doi.org/10.11647/OBP.0424.00

announcing the start of the battle. Silence prevails, and the air is filled with nervous anticipation.

This is the start of a typical performance. The lead poet of each *jawqa* sings an introductory ode before the successive verbal duels between two poets—one from each *jawqa*—begin. The *riddādeh* sing each poet's last line twice, usually to the accompaniment of musical instruments such as an electric keyboard or a clarinet, and handheld drums and tambourines. The *riddādeh*'s role is important in that they give the poets time to compose and declaim the next lines in the contest.

What happens over the course of the next three to four hours is a battle in words couched in sophisticated musical-metrical improvised compositions. It often revolves around an opposition such as hot and cold, war and peace, youth and old age, and so on. A poet from each *jawqa* takes up one side of the opposition and declaims his lines, much to the amusement of the crowd of enthusiasts on the edge of their seats. Each poet delivers a succession of lines leading to a witty clincher that the audience anticipates and which the chorus repeats to the accompaniment of their musical instruments. Everything is declaimed or sung in well-known metrical and musical metres, highlighting the topics chosen.

This traditional oral art is prevalent throughout the Lebanese mountains and coastal villages and cities, as well as in the large and vibrant Lebanese immigrant communities around the globe. It is the country's most cherished and revered form of entertainment. The huge output of poets accumulated over centuries has been and still is being preserved in print and audio-visual recordings. It is treasured by the Lebanese, old and young alike, who commit their favourite lines to memory and repeat them among friends.

My study explores the metrics of Lebanese *zajal* poetry, its significance and popularity within the broader context of oral traditions in the Arab world and the Mediterranean region. It also discusses the various genres, and the relationship and interplay between metrical and musical metre.

Oral poetry in the Arab world encompasses various forms of oral expression, including storytelling, recitations, and sung poetry. These traditions are characterised by their reliance on the spoken word rather than written text, making them dynamic and adaptable to different contexts.

All twenty-two Arab countries have oral traditions, some more popular than others, which are known by several different names and use different metrical forms. In Saudi Arabia and the Arabian Gulf, it is known as Nabati poetry. In Lebanon, Syria, Palestine, and Jordan, one common term for it is *zajal*. It is known as *al-zāmil* in Yemen, *al-malḥūn* in Morocco, *al-zaḥfa* in Mauritania, *al-ḥasja* in Iraq, and *al-dubeit* in the Sudan, to mention only a few. Add to all this the vast oral poetic production of various Bedouin tribes in most, if not all, of the Arab countries, especially in Jordan and Saudi Arabia. Bedouin communities have a rich tradition of oral poetry, often recited during gatherings, celebrations, or as a form of competitive poetic duelling known as *naqāʾid*. Bedouin poets compose verses that reflect their nomadic lifestyle, values, and genealogy. These poems are not only artistic but also serve as a means of documenting the history and lineage of their tribes.

It is the diglossic nature of Arabic, the formal written and the informal spoken tradition, that explains the presence, variety, and popularity of oral poetry throughout the Arab world. The enormous variation in cultural settings and norms, as well as geographic milieu, also plays an important role in explaining the diverse nature of oral poetry traditions around the Arab world. While an in-depth comparative study of these similarities and differences is not the focus of this study, further exploration along such lines is certainly warranted.

One aspect to consider is the parallel between Lebanese *zajal* and other vernacular poetic traditions in the Arab world. Similar challenges faced by Lebanese poets in terms of scansion and metre have been addressed in the study of the Nabati poetry of Arabia and surrounding regions. Scholars such as Saad Abdullah Sowayan and Marcel Kurpershoek have made significant contributions to understanding these poetic traditions. Sowayan, in his seminal work *Nabati Poetry: The Oral Poetry of Arabia* (1985), provides a detailed metrical analysis that reveals a complex system of 51 different metres grouped into 14 classes.[1] These metres, while distinct from their Classical Arabic counterparts, share some resemblances and highlight the necessity for scholars to consider the unique linguistic and performative contexts of vernacular poetry.

---

[1] See the chapter on 'Prosody and Language: A Synchronic and Diachronic Overview' in Sowayan 1985, 147–67.

Sowayan's insights are particularly relevant, as they emphasise the importance of auditory validation in vernacular poetry. Nabati poets, much like Lebanese *zajal* poets, assess the metrical soundness of their verses through recitation and singing. This approach underscores the necessity of understanding the performance context and the oral nature of these poetic forms.

Beyond the contemporary Arab world, a similar oral tradition to the Lebanese tradition is that of the *zajals* of Ibn Quzmān (d. 1160) in al-Andalus, the Muslim-ruled parts of the Iberian Peninsula, which still suffer from the ongoing debate over the metrical system of Hispano-Arabic poetry.[2] The opponents and proponents of the purely quantitative or the purely syllabic accentual approach to the *zajals* and the *muwashshaḥāt*[3] of al-Andalus have been seeking easy solutions to a problem that may very well prove quite complex and formidable. Unfortunately, the

---

[2] The major controversy over the metrical system of Andalusian strophic poetry dates back to the nineteenth century and continues through the twentieth to the present. One group of scholars, represented by García Gómez, argued for a stress-syllabic basis for the *zajals* of Ibn Quzmān. Other scholars questioned this stress-syllabic approach and argued instead for the workings of a quantitative system. See Hartmann 1897; García Gómez 1972; Corriente 1980; and Monroe's extensive writings on Andalusian poetry, especially 'Which Came First, the *Zajal* or the *Muwashshaḥa*?' (1989); and the preface and introduction to his *Hispano-Arabic Poetry* (1974). Also see note 5 below.

[3] The *muwashshaḥa* (pl. *muwashshaḥāt*) is a strophic poem originating from al-Andalus consisting of several divisions with particular rhyme schemes that differ from author to author and ending with a *kharja*. (See note below for the definition of *kharja*.)

dialects in question are sketchily known only through reconstructions based on a limited number of texts and have been treated as parts of two different and rarely complementary scholarly enterprises. In the case of the *zajals*, the *muwashshaḥāt*, and especially the *kharjas*,[4] a careful account of the music to which these poetical compositions were sung is indispensable for determining their prosodic features. Again, unfortunately, our knowledge of the music is elementary and insufficient. Most of the music was not written down and the notations that exist are hard to decipher. Therefore, all emendations, textual analyses and even studies based on hypothetical common Romance lyrical prototypes must remain tentative and exploratory. These approaches cannot replace the crucial dialectal and musical considerations that inform the poetry.[5]

Through the application of the methodologies employed in my study and in light of those used by scholars of neighbouring traditions, we can gain a more nuanced understanding of the challenges and solutions related to the scansion and metrics of vernacular poetry. This comparative perspective enriches our

---

[4] *Kharja* refers to the concluding *bayt* ('verse') of a *muwashshaḥa*, mostly in colloquial diction, often expressing a love theme.

[5] Monroe makes an excellent and convincing case for the relationship between Romance and Arabic love poetry, and consequently the influence of the Ibero-Romance stress-syllabic meters on the prosody of the Arabic and Hebrew *muwashshaḥāt* to which Romance *kharjas* are appended. See especially his 'Formulaic Diction and the Common Origins of Romance Lyric Traditions' (1975) and 'Studies on the *Ḫarǧas*' (1977). Also, see Monroe and Swialto 1977.

appreciation of *zajal* and situates it within the broader landscape of Arabic oral traditions.

In addition to their aesthetic qualities, the metrics of *zajal* serve as a mnemonic device, aiding poets in the composition and recitation of lengthy verses. The repetitive and predictable patterns of metre and rhyme allow poets to weave complex narratives without losing their audience's attention. This rhythmic consistency also enables the audience to anticipate and participate in the performance, blurring the lines between performer and spectator. The communal aspect of *zajal*, therefore, is not only a cultural phenomenon but also a linguistic and metrical strategy that enhances the overall impact of the poetry.

In summary, Lebanese *zajal* poetry shares several fundamental characteristics with other Arab and Mediterranean oral poetry traditions, such as the emphasis on orality, improvisation, use of local dialects, thematic content, and the role of music and cultural identity. These commonalities underscore the rich and interconnected heritage of oral poetry throughout the Arab world and the Mediterranean region, reflecting the enduring relevance and adaptability of these traditions in the modern world. This book aims to shed light on the intricate artistry behind Lebanese *zajal* poetry by exploring its genres and metrics. Through detailed analysis and contextual exploration, readers will gain a deeper appreciation for the skill and creativity that define Lebanese *zajal*, as well as its significance in the broader landscape of Arabic literature. In doing so, it also acknowledges the valuable contributions of scholars who have studied similar traditions, thereby situating Lebanese *zajal* within a wider scholarly discourse.

1. TERMS AND METHODOLOGY

The study that follows raises important issues and suggests solutions to the tradition of Lebanese *zajal* poetry which shares with its Andalusian counterpart a vernacular Arabic idiom, a common Arabic literary heritage and numerous formal characteristics. The study argues that a thorough knowledge of dialect and music is the key to scansion rules and metrical description, a fact which may offer critics of Hispano-Arabic poetry a new and necessary focus and direction. Fortunately, such knowledge is attainable in the now living tradition of Lebanese vernacular poetry.

In its Hispano-Arabic context the term *zajal* describes a strophic form entirely in the vernacular idiom which bears a close structural relationship to that of the *muwashshaḥa*. In the Lebanese tradition it means primarily oral vernacular poetry in general, a discourse in many forms, composed in or for performance, declaimed or sung to the accompaniment of music. It is also used to characterise a written tradition which attains high literary value and high formal virtuosity in the compositions of famous Lebanese poets writing either exclusively in the vernacular[1] or in both the vernacular and the literary language (*fuṣḥā*).[2] Critics have only begun to assess the influence of *zajal* poetics on major

[1] 'Vernacular' is used here to designate colloquial Lebanese diction as it is spoken today in various parts of Lebanon, in parts of Syria, Jordan and Palestine.

[2] *Fuṣḥā* refers both to Classical Arabic as well as to Modern Standard Arabic.

https://doi.org/10.11647/OBP.0424.01

modern Lebanese poets and consequently on the form and content of modern Lebanese and Arabic poetry in *fuṣḥā*.[3]

The etymology of *zajal* points clearly to song and music. The verb *zajala* means 'to raise the voice in singing, to produce a sweet, pleasing melody'.[4] As a genre of poetry, *zajal* is closely associated with *muʿannā* (or *maʿannā*), a term predating *zajal* but often used interchangeably with it to designate vernacular Lebanese poetry (*al-shiʿr al-ʿāmmī, al-shiʿr al-shaʿbī, al-shiʿr al-qawmī,* or *al-shiʿr al-lubnānī*) in its entirety. Anīs Frayḥa derives *maʿannā* from the Syriac word *ʿannī* 'to sing',[5] the term itself being a passive participial form of the root. Others disagree with Frayḥa's etymology, although they still relate the term to Syriac origin,[6] despite the fact that its derivation from the second form of the Arabic root *ʿ-n-y* is quite legitimate linguistically. At any rate, the Syriac derivation associates the term *maʿannā* with singing, while that of the Arabic emphasises the semantic meaning of *ʿannā* 'to

[3] See, for example, Jayyusi 1977, 252–53.

[4] Ibn Manẓūr 1994, XI:301–2.

[5] See Whaybeh 1952, 63, where Whaybeh quotes from a letter sent to him by Frayḥa. Also see Frayḥa 1973, 173 and 1957, 273. Note that *ʿannī* derives from the proto-Semitic *ghanaya* 'to sing'.

[6] "The term *maʿannā* is derived from the Syriac word *maʿanīshu* (or song)." (See Whaybeh 1952, 63, where he quotes from a letter dated 28 December 1950, sent to him by ʿĪsā Iskandar al-Maʿlūf.) Syriac experts see this etymology as unlikely, and instead argue for the possible derivation of *maʿannā* from the Syriac word *maʿnīthā* 'chant, antiphon'. See Brockelmann 1928, 533.

cause to be emaciated as a result of love'.[7] This, in the opinion of Amīn Nakhleh, for example, accounts for the preponderance of love themes in early manifestations of Lebanese vernacular poetry.[8]

Whatever the case, during the past fifty years *zajal* has replaced *maʿannā* as the term for this poetry. *Maʿannā* has reverted to the designation of a particular subgenre and a particular metre[9] used extensively, though not exclusively, in verbal duels, while *zajal* seems to have acquired, at least till the late 1940s in the little known but numerous compositions of Lebanese immigrants in the United States,[10] the name of a specific metre that differentiated it from *maʿannā* and other metres.

The poet of *zajal* is called *zajjāl*, *qawwāl*, or *shāʿir*. While the three terms are often used interchangeably, there are clear and basic differences between their meanings. *Zajjāl* is strictly speaking a composer of *zajal* who may or may not be capable of improvisation or extemporisation,[11] and who may or may not

---

[7] See ʿAwwād 1930, 441, quoting an unpublished book manuscript by ʿĪsā Iskandar al-Maʿlūf entitled *Nayl al-mutamannā fī fann al-maʿannā*.

[8] See Nakhleh 1945, 39.

[9] Nakhleh 1945, pp. 37–39.

[10] See, for example, Kafrkadī 1942, 71, 105, 115, 121.

[11] The interesting question of improvisation and extemporization is dealt with in my 1989 article on verbal duelling. Though the two terms are defined in the same manner in most dictionaries, extemporization, unlike improvisation, involves prior preparation. In most verbal duels in Lebanon, the poets agree in advance on the general topic for which they will prepare prior to the duel. During the duel they then improvise whenever specific arguments require quick responses.

attain in his compositions a level of literary excellence to merit the name of a *shāʿir* ('poet'). Like the *qawwāl*, the *zajjāl*'s main function is *iṣābat al-maʿnā*, a phrase best translated as 'doing justice to the meaning' or 'treating a subject in the most efficient way possible in order to convey an intended message'. The emphasis in the word *qawwāl* is on *qawl*, i.e., 'uttering, declaiming, or singing',[12] on improvisation or extemporization in particular social functions. The *qawwāl* is also referred to as *ibn al-kār* ('man of the trade'), *ibn al-fann* ('master of the art'), or *ibn al-dhakā* ('*bel-esprit*'),[13] all of which are clearly value-laden terms. Mostly uneducated, though in many cases literate, the *qawwāls* are highly respected by the people of their villages and towns and are sought out to recite *zajals* on religious holidays, political celebrations, births, christenings, marriages, and funerals. Those whose fame reaches beyond their immediate region are called upon to duel other *qawwāls* or suffer loss of prestige among their critical public.[14] The term *shāʿir al-zajal* is principally reserved to the written vernacular which in the hands of poets such as Michel Ṭrād, William Ṣaʿb, and Asʿad Sābā has preserved this predominantly oral tradition in literary masterpieces. *Shāʿir* is not, however, exclusively the provenance of the written vernacular, for the better

---

[12] *Qawl* is another name for Lebanese *zajal* poetry. See Nakhleh 1945, 39. For the association of *qawl* with singing, see Frayḥa 1957, 274.

[13] Cf. Nakhleh, 1945, 39, and Lecerf 1932, 219.

[14] On the prestige accorded to the *qawwāls* and the critical audience involved in verbal duels see Lecerf 1932, 219–20, and Frayḥa 1957, 274–77.

qawwāls and *zajjāls* have, while observing their main function, that of *iṣābat al-maʿnā*, produced highly sophisticated poetry.

The foregoing statements are intended to introduce briefly Lebanese *zajal* and its practitioners, as well as to define basic terms necessary for the metrical analysis that follows. Although no attempt is made to supply a thorough historical background,[15] the study is conscious of historical continuum, and historical questions relevant to the development of *zajal* metrics, and these will be duly highlighted in their proper places.

Throughout, the method used is based on some fifty tapes of *zajal* recorded from live performances, most of the extant *dīwāns* of major poets, spanning a period from the earliest recorded *zajals* until the present, selected poems taped by well-known poets, interviews, and musical analysis and transcriptions of the metres and several Maronite Church hymns.[16] In all cases, the written material notwithstanding, scansion is based on texts declaimed or sung by more than one *zajal* poet.

The study assumes a musical basis for the rendition of all the metres, which, as will be shown momentarily, determines in various degrees all syllable count and much of metrical rhythm. This assumption is borne out by the fact that the poets are usually unconscious of metre as a regulating force and instead intuit metrical form and rhythm from a well-versed knowledge of various

---

[15] For incomplete accounts of the historical background of Lebanese *zajal* see Abdel-Nour 1957, 15–37, and ʿĪsā Iskandar al-Maʿlūf's *Nayl al-mutamannā fī fann al-maʿannā* (unpublished manuscript kept, along with the author's numerous works, with the al-Maʿlūf family in Lebanon).

[16] The church hymns in question were recorded during church services.

musical tunes associated with the various metres. This almost total ignorance of metre is the norm in oral poetry rather than the exception.[17] In the Arabic *fuṣḥā* tradition, for example, metrical rules are culled from the pre-Islamic period of poetry when the poets recited or sang their poetry according to musical rhythms that they intuitively felt suitable to their ears and the ears of their audience. Al-Khalīl's (d. 786) metrical description, ingenious as it was, became a prescription for subsequent poetic practice and may have had a detrimental effect on much of Abbasid poetry which lacked, especially in the hands of secondary poets, the musicality and rhythmic quality characteristic of pre-Islamic poetry in general. In metrics, as in language, one can perhaps speak of a 'langue' and a 'parole', to borrow two of de Saussure's privileged terms. 'Langue' in metrics is similar to al-Khalīl's theoretical system, while 'parole' is the actual practice of an Imruʾ al-Qays or Ṭarafa Ibn al-ʿAbd, for example. The first is general and theoretical; the latter is empirical and particular. This analysis is a description of the 'parole' of vernacular Lebanese poetry, a first but essential step to the formalist who wishes to generate the rules governing this poetry. As 'langue', al-Khalīl's system will be shown incapable of accounting for many of the formal characteristics of *fuṣḥā* poetry. This is important since al-Khalīl's system is utilised in the description of some but not all *zajal* metres. Therefore, when it is used, it will be duly modified.

The limited written poetry used here is unwritten in the sense that it is in each case recited or sung in order to determine

---

[17] Cf. Lord 1960.

the relationship between syllable count, alternation of feet (when these clearly exist), and stress patterns where relevant, and in order to eliminate misreading resulting from unstable and often whimsical transcription practices. The difficulty of reading *zajals* stems from the fact that the graphemes of *fuṣḥā* Arabic which are used in transcription are totally inadequate. In using such graphemes, particular attention is paid to the morphology of *fuṣḥā* words, usually at the high expense of slurring or lengthening certain syllables.

Note, for example, that *yā ahl al-hawā* (‘O, people of love’) is written in the following configuration: *yā*, a vocative particle; *ahl*, a construct noun followed by the genitive noun *al-hawā*. In the dialect, the phrase has several possible readings. It could be read as *yahl il-hawā*, basically as two words joined by a *waṣla* (‘liaison’). Morphologically, *yahl*, if written as pronounced, will resemble a verb in the imperfect and will destroy the meaning of the phrase. Clearly, the written language compromises the pronunciation of the phrase to create readable *fuṣḥā* diction, which almost destroys the phrase’s meaning. Read as normally written, *yā ahl al-hawā* with the mandatory *waṣl* between the two nouns in the genitive construction, yields the following syllable pattern: _ _ _ ⏑ _.[18] Read as often pronounced, *yahl il-hawā*, it gives: _ _ ⏑ _, one syllable less than the former. Appearing in another metre, the phrase may indeed have to be read as *yā ahl-lil-hawā*, _ _ _ ⏑ _, but there is no way of determining which way of reading is appropriate from the undiscriminating text. Add to this

[18] Note that scansion should be read from left to right throughout the work.

the reading possibilities that the dialect itself allows and the problems multiply.

To illustrate, consider the phrase *yā bint ʿammī*[19] ('O, my uncle's daughter'), which a native speaker can read as *yā bint ʿammī*, _ _o _ _, or as *yā binti ʿammī*, _ _ ⏑ _ _, or as *yā binit ʿammī*, _ ⏑ _ _ _, or even *yā bnit ʿammī*, _ _ _ _, each reading of which may be called for in only one metrical situation. The solution to such complex possibilities determines our ability to describe the metres of *zajal* and at the same time points to one of the problems that face the writers on other Arabic vernacular *zajals* where an inadequate knowledge of dialect exists. A related problem has to do with extra-long syllables as in the example above *yā bint ʿammī*. Here, *bint* is an extra-long syllable which in some metres may be treated as roughly equal to a long syllable, while in others it is given the value of a long and a short, whether it is declaimed as *bint* or *bint*[*i*]. In such frequent cases, music and song may present a key to scansion.

The importance of oral rendition is further highlighted by the role that the music and the *jawqa* ('chorus') play in scanning the lines of particular metres where the chorus repeats specific lines or hemistichs at specific intervals. This practice is employed in parts of verbal duels, for example, where choral repetition of lines gives the *zajjāl* time to prepare his answer to his opponent's argument. What is of interest here is the particular way, the

19 Henceforth, an extra-long syllable is designated by _o.

particular intonation, with which the chorus sings the lines. To illustrate, consider the following line:[20]

Yā Qays ḥājī tzīd ʿā Laylā ṣdūd

_ _o _ _ _o _ _ _ _o

'Qays, stop increasing your estrangement from Laylā'

This line, when read or declaimed, consists of six long syllables and three extra-long ones (*Qays*, *tzīd*, and *ṣdūd*), yet when sung, three short syllables appear, one after the first two extra-long syllables and one, as a short vowel, at the beginning of the third. A *waṣla*, moreover, is added to affect liaison between *hājī* and *tzīd* after the *ī* in *hājī* is shortened. The resulting scansion is

Yā Qays[i] ḥājī tzīd[i] ʿā Laylā ṣ[i]dūd

_ _ ᴗ _ _ _ ᴗ _ _ _ ᴗ _

It resembles a shorter form of the *fuṣḥā* metre *al-rajaz* (_ _ ᴗ _ / _ _ ᴗ _ / _ _ ᴗ _) which has the basic foot *mustafʿilun* (_ _ ᴗ _).

Likewise, the following line from a famous verbal duel[21] is declaimed as:

[W]-min mayl tānī [b]yidhikrak marʾet tarī

_ _o _ _ ᴗ _ _ _ _ ᴗ _o

'And from another angle it (history) will mention you briefly'

Min ḥayth lāzim yidhkur il-ghannā maʿī

_ _o _ _ _ ᴗ _ _ _ ᴗ _

'Because it (history) must mention these who sang with me'

---

[20] This is a well-known line by Joseph al-Hāshim (pen name: Zaghlūl al-Dāmūr).

[21] The reference is to the encounter between Zaghlūl al-Dāmūr's group and Mūsā Zghayb's group at Deir al-Qalʿa in the village of Beit Mirī, Lebanon, in 1971. More than 10,000 people attended the duel.

Yet, when the last hemistich is sung by the chorus, a short vowel is inserted after *ḥayth* producing a pattern of feet resembling the typical *rajaz* of al-Khalīl's system:

> *Min ḥayth[i] lāzim yidhkur il-ghannā maʿī*
>
> — — ⏑ — — — ⏑ — — — ⏑ —

or — — ⏑ — / — — ⏑ — / — — ⏑ —. When and where short syllables are inserted seems connected with a particular tune associated with a particular metre and of this more will be discussed in the course of this analysis.

The problem of reading printed *zajals* is compounded by the difficult choice of how and which words or parts of words enter into metrical scansion. In the first hemistich of the line cited above, the conjunction *wāw* ('and') is not voiced by the poet, although its meaning is essential to the meaning of the whole line. Since the poetry is declaimed or sung, only what is heard counts in metrical scansion. In other instances and other metres, the *wāw* may indeed be voiced as *wa* or *wi* or even as *iw*, making it this time around a long syllable. Again, different poets may render a word differently. For instance, one pronounced the word *[b]yidhikrak* (⏑ — —), while another opted for *ʾibyidhkirak* (— ⏑ — —), pausing after the preceding word (*tānī*), and forming a long syllable composed of an added glottal stop *ʾi* and the ensuing unvowelled consonant. Far from being arbitrary, however, such choices point at once to two important principles. On the one hand, they indicate how unreliable the printed text is and, on the other hand and perhaps more importantly, they offer a clue to syllabic variations that do not affect the basic rhythmic pattern of the metre and hence to the rules governing these changes.

In addition to all this, there are many phonetic variations and internal vowel changes that differ from one region in Lebanon to another, and although a great deal of reform has been attempted with the purpose of purging the Lebanese and other Arab dialects of *fuṣḥā* influence,[22] this influence still exists in the appearance of fully inflected words in some *zajals*. All these are important factors in metrical analysis, factors which are at the basis of this work.

Yet, assuming that there are lines in which these factors play a minimal role, there is nevertheless the danger of jumping into facile conclusions concerning the whole poem or whole poems, as is the case unfortunately in the partial and highly selective efforts of most Lebanese *zajal* critics.[23] It is not difficult to single out a few lines or a few poems and arrive at a conclusion that does not have universal applicability, as the discussion later on will show. One danger is to take little or no cognizance of oral rendition and instead depend on the more regularised productions of literate poets, though oral factors are very much in evidence in the works of the better literate poets. It is not unusual, for example, for several lines in any one poem to have great variation in the number of syllables, but these variations are not always related to the formal characteristics of the metre to which they belong. They may simply be due to problems of recitation

---

[22] See Abdel-Nour 1957, 81–91.

[23] To mention only a few, Munīr Whaybeh, Tawfīq ʿAwwād, Jabbūr ʿAbd al-Nūr (Jabbour Abdel-Nour), and Ibrāhīm al-Ḥūrānī 1906, 602–4.

where the apparent absence of a syllable at the beginning of a line could be easily rectified by appealing to a 'carry over' from the singing of the line that precedes it. This is a crucial observation which has gone so far unheeded, one which has caused premature assumptions about metre in general.

The foregoing remarks clearly show that knowledge of the dialect by itself will not divulge the metrical pattern or the number of syllables in Lebanese *zajal* metres. Music seems to play a corrective role integral to proper scansion. The chorus in *zajals* where there is choral accompaniment will be shown to set down a regular pattern which enables us to locate where syllables should be inserted and hence to study the reasons for the extent and limitation of the poet's own execution of metre. In brief, there appear to be two ways of scanning a line of *zajal*: one derived from reading aloud or declaiming; the other from music and song. The first one will be proven below to be inconsistent; the other more stable and more pertinent to a sung poetic tradition.

Although it is not customary to admit stress into discussions of Arabic metrics, since al-Khalīl did not, according to most commentators on his metrical system, specifically use the term or admit clearly the workings of stress patterns, an argument will be made here for the integral role that stress plays both in Arabic *fuṣḥā* metres, as well as in *zajal*. It goes without saying that it is inconceivable in an oral sung tradition to produce purely quantitative or, for that matter, purely qualitative verse. How the poet reads or sings his lines, his intonations, rising or falling rhythms, pitches, in sum, his peculiar and unique delivery, all point to the presence of stress. Here again musical accent will help us locate metrical stress and arrive at metrical description with certainty. In his important comparative study of *fuṣḥā* metrics,[24] Kamāl Abū Dīb discusses in great detail the role that *al-nabr* ('stress') plays in the rhythm of Arabic poetry, and further reference to his findings will be made in the work at hand. Any study, it seems to me, which treats Arabic metres as simply quantitative is bound to fail. The confusion and lack of consensus concerning the scansion of many poems from the Arabic *fuṣḥā* tradition, that still plague the students of Arabic *fuṣḥā* poetry, are precisely the product of such a simplistic approach. Any attempt, therefore, to modify the metres of Lebanese *zajal* to suit a purely quantitative system, as al-Khalīl's system was understood to be, will lead nowhere. Indeed, the very attempt to hold al-Khalīl's system as a measuring rod for vernacular metres, as many have done,[25] shows an unjustified levelling of differences between the *fuṣḥā* and the vernacular. When it is remembered that Arabic dialects in general share the important feature of dropping desinential inflections and most internal vowels with the ensuing erosion of a large number of short syllables and the increase in extra-long syllables, it becomes clear that we are dealing with a new morphology which differs significantly from the *fuṣḥā*, its rhythms and its stress patterns. To hope then that a metrical system based on limited syllabic configurations derived from the formal characteristics of the root system in *fuṣḥā* could somehow be tailored to describe the

---

[24] Abū Dīb 1974.

[25] See, for example, Abdel-Nour 1957, 97. Whaybeh, on the other hand, is neither aware of quantity nor stress.

morphology of a parallel vernacular system is untenable and unscholarly. Nor can any appeal to *ziḥāf*[26] and *iʿlāl*[27] surmount the difficulty or present a serious alternative. Vernacular metrics must answer to the morphology of vernacular poetry. This does not mean that metres in the vernacular may not resemble, and, at times, coincide with some of the ideal Khalilian metres, but the resemblance in those cases will be a direct consequence of morphological similarities between the vernacular and those particular metres. The study then will make no such assumptions. Each metre will be described separately with deference to the dialect and the music employed. In those metres where a case could be made for a *fuṣḥā* prototype, the various 'licences' which are inadmissible in *fuṣḥā* will be cited and discussed.

Finally, the study of oral poetry is fraught with questions about the role of improvisation, composition-cum-recitation, memory, formulaic content, and contact between poet and audience. These questions assume significance or lack of significance in various manifestations of *zajal* poetry and their function is a good topic for another work. In a study of metrics, however, they serve to explain rare inconsistencies in certain metres where the

---

[26] *Ziḥāf* (pl. *ziḥāfāt*; 'relaxation') is, as the name suggests, minor deviations from the ideal feet of a particular meter. The *ziḥāfāt* cause a small quantitative change in the weak syllables in the poetic foot. See Weil 1986, 671.

[27] *Iʿlāl* (lit. 'diseases', 'defects') are major deviations affecting only the last foot in the hemistich. When they appear, they do so in the same form and the same position in all the lines in the poem. See Weil 1986, 671.

oral poet, constrained by the speed of compositions, compromises his metre and his rhythm. When found at all, these inconsistencies appear mainly in verbal duels where improvisation and a demanding audience put inordinate demands on the poet's 'correctness'. A careful account of some of these has been done for this study and has proved of no consequence to metrical description, since they are usually pointed out and repudiated by the poets themselves.[28] They are mentioned here in order to caution critics of Lebanese *zajal* against attributing to them important value. The question as to why they appear in verbal duels is of great relevance to the object of this study. As will become clear later on, the metres involved are characterised when sung by a freer musical realization than that of other metres where the beats take on a rigid neutral pattern superimposed upon the natural language.

---

[28] In the course of assembling the material for this work, I came across a few instances where a dueller repudiates his opponents for jarring the rhythm. Such repudiations are part of the dueller's strategy to undermine the strength of the opponent's argument, but the readiness with which they are spotted points to the poets' consciousness of 'correct' rhythm.

2. PREVIOUS SCHOLARSHIP ON *ZAJAL* METRICS

The scholarship that exists on the metrics of Lebanese *zajal* is almost entirely text-oriented, often consisting of impressionistic statements based on the scansion of a few lines. Much of it does not make claim to metrical analysis and pays lip service to the problem by listing without discrimination or argumentation the previous fragmentary and often opposing views of critics on the subject. Documentation is drastically lacking and, when it exists at all, it is too general or refers to obscure works which are out of print, or lost, or in hard-to-find manuscripts.[1] In general, writers on *zajal* tend to avoid metrics and concentrate instead on historical, biographical, or folkloristic considerations which are important but are rarely utilised to contribute to metrical studies. Formal considerations, such as rhyme and verse form are usually presented as alternatives to analyses of metre and rhythm. In fact, metre is described by many as a rhyme pattern or a particular configuration of verbal tricks, as when diacritics appear on every letter of every word in the poem or where the first letters of every

[1] In many scholarly articles written in Arabic, one is struck by the complete lack of footnotes. The author of this work has tried in vain to locate a reference to the work of a monk known as Anṭūn al-Balīgh, which was, according to Whaybeh 1952, 31–32, published in 1909 by the Maronite Patriarch al-Raḥmānī. In those cases where manuscripts on metrics could be located, the works turned out to be specifically about Syriac poetry.

 https://doi.org/10.11647/OBP.0424.02

line follow alphabetical order.[2] If the metre is recognised at all, it is usually left unnamed or at best acknowledged as different from another unnamed metre.

The most quoted account of *zajal* poetry is Amīn Nakhleh's introduction to *Maʿannā Rashīd Nakhleh* (1945). Both Amīn and his father, Rashīd, were accomplished *fuṣḥā* poets, the latter having completely abandoned *fuṣḥā* poetry in favour of *zajal* and earned himself the title of 'Prince of the *Maʿannā*' (*amīr al-maʿannā*)[3] for the many *zajal* forms that he invented. The introduction to the book makes it clear that the history of the various Arabic *zajal* traditions is fragmentary, usually consisting of classifications based on subject matter and form. Nowhere in the previous scholarship he cites is an attempt made to attribute to poetic metre or poetic structure a semantic value or a role in the classifications. An account of some of these is in order here.

Al-Muḥibbī (d. 1699),[4] for example, divides vernacular poetry into five *aqsām* ('parts' or 'divisions'), one of which is termed *zajal* because it treats *ghazal* ('love poetry'), uses flower and wine imagery, and dwells on personal emotions. The other four are *balīq*, which employs jests and licentious topics, *ḥamāq*, which uses satire and jokes, *muzaylij*, which mixes *fuṣḥā* with colloquialisms, and *mukaffir*, which contains aphorisms and sermons.[5]

---

[2] For a full account of such verbal tricks see al-Fighālī 1939, 15–25. Also see Whaybeh 1952, 63–81.

[3] In 1933 the General Assembly of the Lebanese *zajal* poets conferred the title upon Rashīd Nakhleh. See Abdel-Nour 1957, 69.

[4] 1873, I:108.

[5] Al-Muḥibbī 1873, I:108.

Clearly, the classification here depends entirely on content. Al-Ibshīhī (d. 1448),[6] on the other hand, lists seven *funūn*, ('genres; constituent arts?'): *al-shiʿr al-qarīḍ* ('*fuṣḥā* poetry'), *al-muwashshaḥ*, *al-dubayt*,[7] *al-zajal*, *al-mawāliyyāt*,[8] *al-kān wa-kān*,[9] and *al-qūmā*,[10] the last four of which are in the vernacular idiom. In addition, he recognises *al-ḥamāq* and *al-mūsijān* which he does not define. Whether these vernacular genres are characterised by particular metrical configurations or are differentiated according to form and content is not made clear. In a similar vein, Ṣafiyy al-Dīn al-Ḥillī (d. 1349)[11] speaks of four *funūn* without much elaboration. Only Ibn Khaldūn (d. 1406) views *zajal* as a method of composition which, according to him, predates the *muwashshaḥ* and uses the vernacular in all the fifteen Khalīlian

---

[6] 1900, II:267–68.

[7] *Al-dubayt* consists of two verses (four hemistichs) with the rhyme scheme a a b a. See al-Ibshīhī 1900, II:261.

[8] For an etymology of *mawāliyya* (pl. *mawāliyyāt*) see Cachia 1977, 77–103.

[9] See al-Ibshīhī's *al-Mustaṭraf* for examples of this genre. Also see al-Muḥibbī 1873, I:108–10. The name *al-kān wa-kān* suggests that the content of poems in this genre relate an anecdote or give a sermon. In other words, a *kān wa-kān* poem relates what was (or *mā kān*). See Whaybeh 1952, 61.

[10] It is said that *al-qūmā* derived its name from the call of Baghdadi singers: *qūmā li nasḥur qūmā* ('rise and let us have a light meal before daybreak'). The reference is to *al-suḥūr* ('the light meal before daybreak') during the month of Ramaḍān. See al-Muḥibbī 1873, I:108.

[11] Al-Ḥillī 1983, 5.

metres.[12] Though admitting that these vernacular genres have specific *awzān* ('metrical forms'), most of the critics are content to leave it at that or specify that most of these *awzān* are different from those used by the Arabs in *fuṣḥā* poetry. Even those who see a close relationship between vernacular and *fuṣḥā* metres merely gloss over the fact or evade close analysis.

The situation is not much different with Amīn Nakhleh. He too, despite his thoroughness, avoids metrical analysis and involves the reader in a terminological jungle erasing the distinction between *zajal* structures and *zajal* metres. According to him, Lebanese *zajal*, "[o]ne of the many extant old *zajal* traditions *(farʿ min tilka al-ṭarāʾiq al-qadīma)*, is none other than Lebanese *maʿannā*."[13] Having said that, he divides *maʿannā* into four *anwāʿ* ('kinds, genres?'):[14] *al-maṭlaʿ* (lit., the opening), also called *al-maʿannā al-ʿādī* ('the usual [common] *maʿannā*'), *al-badāli* ('the alternate one'), which differs from *al-maṭlaʿ* in metre, *al-muwashshaḥ*, which again differs in metre from *al-maṭlaʿ*, and *al-qaṣīd* ('the ode?') which employs either the *wāfir* metre of al-Khalīl (presumably without modification), or the metre of *al-maṭlaʿ*, or that of *al-badāli*. What the metres of *al-maṭlaʿ* and *al-badāli* are, we are not told. Nakhleh instead devotes his efforts to the various rhyme patterns in which each of the four *anwāʿ* appears in the written tradition, especially in the *dīwān* of Rashīd Nakhleh who is credited with the invention of most of these

[12] See Ibn Khaldūn 1969, 458–59.

[13] Nakhleh 1945, 44.

[14] Nakhleh 1945, 44.

patterns.[15] Only one metre, *al-wāfir*, is spelled out and that with a specific reference to *al-badāli* from *Maʿannā Rashīd Nakhleh.*

Zajal, he continues, consists of six *funūn*: *al-muhmal* (which is completely without diacritical marks), *al-marṣūd* (in which the *rawiyy* starts with a particular obligatory letter), *al-mujazzam* (where every line in the successive stanzas rhymes with the others except for the last line whose rhyme is a *rujūʿ* [‘return’] to the rhyme of the opening line or lines), and, finally, *al-alifiyyāt* (in which the first letter of every line follows the order of the Arabic alphabet). In the context, the word *funūn* means something different from genre as al-Ibshīhī’s usage indicates. It describes, rather, a written style characterised by *badīʿ* (figurative language), formal idiosyncrasies, and verbal virtuosity.

Nakhleh then identifies ‘several methods’ (*ʿiddat ṭarāʾiq*).[16] The first one of these is *al-qarrādī*[17] (also pronounced *al-qirrādī*) which in turn subsumes a number of *funūn* such as *karj al-ḥajal* (‘the gait of the partridge’), *mashy al-sitt* (‘the gait of ladies’), *daqq al-miṭraqa* (‘the pounding of the hammer’), *al-murabbaʿ* (‘the quatrain’), *al-mijwiz* (‘the couplet’), *naqlet al-ʿarūs* (‘the moving of the young bride to her husband’s home’), *al-shūfāni* (‘related to the Shūf area in Lebanon’), *al-ʿādī* (‘the usual one‘), *al-muwashshaḥ* (‘the adorned one‘), *al-mukhammas al-mardūd* (’the

[15] See, for example, Nakhleh 1945, 45–51.

[16] Nakhleh 1945, 52.

[17] Amīn Nakhleh calls it *al-qurrādī*, but he could be alone among *zajal* critics. *Qarrādī* and *qirrādī* are used interchangeably in Lebanon today.

quintuplet refrain'),[18] *al-muhmal* ('without diacritics'), and *al-munaqqaṭ* (in which each letter is dotted with diacritics). These *funūn*, this time around, suggest not only rhyme patterns and verbal tricks, but also styles of oral delivery and singing as is made quite clear by the etymology of the first four. Moreover, among the *ṭarāʾiq* of *zajal*, Nakhleh lists two kinds of *ḥidā*[19] with various rhyme patterns, *al-ḥawrabeh* poem,[20] *al-zalāghīt* or *al-zaghārīd*, a form specifically used in wedding celebrations, *al-nadb* ('elegiac verse'), and *jalwet al-ʿarūs*, a strophic composition sung or recited by women when welcoming a new bride.

In addition to these *anwāʿ*, *funūn*, and *ṭarāʾiq*, Nakhleh lists what he terms *ṭarāʾiq ʿāmmiyya qadīma* ('old vernacular methods'):[21] *ʿatābā*, *mījanā*, and *abū al-zuluf*[22] which he treats under *bāb al-aghānī*, or sung compositions, and in which, according to him, *naẓm* ('ordered beat') rather than *nagham* ('melody') plays

[18] This refers to one of the many rhyme schemes of *qarrādī*. *Al-mukhammas al-mardūd* usually consists of four-line stanzas (eight hemistichs) that rhyme, a b, a b, a b, a and c, this last rhyme being used throughout the poem. At times a *kharja* is added to the four lines and the rhyme scheme changes to a b, a b, a b, a d and c, with d being an independent rhyme in every one of the stanzas in the poem. See Nakhleh 1945, 54. Note that Whaybeh 1952 gives an example of *mardūd* which differs significantly from that of Nakhleh. His example consists of a *maṭlaʿ* and a *dawr* that rhyme as follows: *maṭlaʿ*, a b, a b; *dawr*, c d, c d, c d, c b. See Whaybeh 1952, 73–74.

[19] See Nakhleh 1945, 56–57.

[20] Or *ḥawraba*, Nakhleh 1945, 57–58.

[21] Nakhleh 1945, 60.

[22] Nakhleh 1945, 60.

the central role. "Also included, under Lebanese *zajal* is *al-shrūqī* (or *al-shurūqī*), known too as *al-qaṣīd al-badawī* ('the Bedouin *qaṣīd*'), and *al-mawwāl al-baghdādī*," two *ṭarāʾiq*, one may surmise, which are still in vogue.

Reading Nakhleh's introduction leaves one with the strong impression that Lebanese *zajal* is extremely rich in form and structure, but little is said of whether these *ṭarāʾiq*, *funūn*, *anwāʿ*, and *aqsām* are further distinguished in terms of metre, or whether metre plays any significant role at all. The arbitrary identification of only some genres with music and singing and the apparent exclusion of others gives, as we shall see, an imperfect picture of the reality of Lebanese *zajal*. After all, this study supplies musical transcriptions for each of the extant metres of *zajal*.

The space that Nakhleh allows for metre in his introduction is a mere paragraph which states categorically that

> Lebanese vernacular poetry in its various *ṭarāʾiq* is predicated upon an aural rhythm, not upon restricted feet. It (i.e., *zajal*) is in its rhythm (*wazn*), in the articulation of sound, the position of vowels (*ḥarakāt*), the structures of words and phrases (*tarākīb al-alfāẓ*), their pronunciation and writing (*sic*) dependent on melody (*nagham*). Some (my emphasis) of its melodies (or rhythms) may be related to the Khalīlian metres.[23]

Important and authoritative as this statement is, it tells us precious little about *zajal* metres and seems to contradict Nakhleh's statements concerning the partial role of music. Moreover, we are not told which "melodies may be related to the Khalīlian

[23] Nakhleh 1945, 67–68.

metres." The rest of Nakhleh's account of metre consists simply of quoted statements by Lebanese critics taken at face value without discussion.

Other critics are no more circumspect, but full cognizance of their partial pronouncements is necessary, first, because their intuitions are often founded on first-hand knowledge of the tradition; second, because some were *zajal* poets themselves (although this fact alone does not necessarily give them claim to authoritative metrical analysis); and third, because any serious study of *zajal* metrics has to deal thoroughly with the available scholarship.

In *Muḥīṭ al-muḥīṭ* under the root *ʿ-n-y*, Buṭrus al-Bustānī (1819–1883) states that *zajal* poets "depend mostly on rhyme such that they do not care for the appropriateness of language or metre."[24] This opinion is shared by others. Dozy, for example, claims that *zajal* composition requires "unity of rhyme, not unity of metre, and that it (*zajal*) has a number of metres."[25] Similarly, Seybold voices the opinion that this art (*zajal*) is based on the unity of rhyme, not on the unity of metre and is composed according to al-Khalīl's metres.[26] Jurjī Zaydān[27] sees a relationship between some metres of *zajal* and those of al-Khalīl's, but others bear no relationship at all to the known metres in *fuṣḥā*. Zaydān

---

[24] Al-Bustānī 1870, II:1489.

[25] Dozy 1967, I:581.

[26] See Nakhleh 1945, 69, where he quotes *Dāʾirat al-Maʿārif al-Islāmiyya* (Cairo), I:263. I have been unable to consult the first edition of the *Dāʾira* to verify Nakhleh's quotation.

[27] Zaydān 1957, IV:206.

agrees with Ibrāhīm al-Ḥūrānī[28] that *rajaz*, *wāfir*, and *sarīʿ* are the only Khalīlian metres found in Lebanese *zajal*. Al-Ḥūrānī, however, qualifies his statement by observing that these three metres undergo changes which are not permissible in *fuṣḥā* poetry. He does not restrict *zajal* metrics to *rajaz*, *wāfir*, and *sarīʿ*, since he sees these metres used specifically in *maʿannā* as opposed to the *qarrādiyyāt*, "some of which do not follow the known Arabic metres, and some of which produce a *mutadārik* scansion with modifications too."[29] He gives two examples of his own composition of *qarrādī*, one in the "modified" *mutadārik* and the other yielding the unusual combination of feet *mustafʿilun* (_ _ ᴗ _) / *mafʿūlun* (_ _ _):

Min kitir shawʾī laykun // *Jīt rākib ʿā ʾṭār in-nār*
_ ᴗ _[30] _ _ _ _ // _o _ _ _ _ _ _o
'Because of my longing for you' //
'I've come riding on the train of fire'

It consists of three and a half feet of the modified *khabab* (commonly confused with *mutadārik*)[31] in each hemistich, _ ᴗ / _ _ / _ _ / _ // _ _ / _ _ / _ _ / _ (_ ᴗ) and,

Rāḥ ish-shabāb il-ghālī // *Wi-sh-shayb[i] ghayyar ḥālī*
_ _ ᴗ _ _ _ _ // _ _ ᴗ _ _ _ _
'Cherished youth has gone by' //
'And hoariness has changed my state'

---

[28] Al-Ḥūrānī 1906, 602–4.

[29] Al-Ḥūrānī 1906, 603.

[30] *Kitir* (ᴗ _) or the permissible *kitri* (_ ᴗ).

[31] _ _ ᴗ _ (*mustafʿilun*) repeated six times constitutes a *bayt* of *rajaz*. Rhythm should be the determining factor in metrical description.

where supposedly a strict *khabab* scansion is not possible due to the position of the short syllable at the beginning of the second foot. At this point, all that can be said is that al-Ḥūrānī has little or no conception of feet except in terms of the *fuṣḥā* metres. His choice in the second *qarrādī* example of _ _ ᴗ _ as a foot rather than dividing the foot into _ _ and ᴗ _, for instance, points first to an arbitrariness not uncommon among students of *fuṣḥā* metrics (when a particular order of syllables coincides with well-known *fuṣḥā* feet), and second to complete unawareness of rhythm.[32]

"As for their [the Lebanese] songs," al-Ḥūrānī adds, "known to them as *al-mawwālāt al-baghdādiyya, al-mawwālāt al-miṣriyya*, and *al-zalāghīṭ*, they are of the *basīṭ* metre...,"[33] although, as he puts it, *al-zalāghīṭ* may exhibit the pattern *mustafʿilun / faʿlān* (_ _ ᴗ _ / _ $\_{o}$), the last syllable being extra-long, as in the following example:

Ghannā ḥamām il-bān // *ʿĀ māyili l-aghṣān*
_ _ ᴗ _ _ $\_{o}$ // _ _ ᴗ _ _ $\_{o}$
'The doves of the ben trees sang' //
'On the swaying branches'

Lammā tamāyal ʾadd // *ʿArūsina r-rayyān*
_ _ ᴗ _ _ $\_{o}$ // ᴗ _ ᴗ _ _ $\_{o}$
'When the figure swayed' //
'The mellow figure of our young bride'

or, _ _ ᴗ _ / _ $\_{o}$ // ᴗ _ ᴗ _ /_ $\_{o}$, repeated twice.

---

[32] Al-Ḥūrānī 1906, 604.

[33] This is a mere conjecture not supported by any proof.

Finally, al-Ḥūrānī continues, "the rest of their songs use the metres of *fuṣḥā* poetry and other metres,"[34] meaning perhaps not quantitative metres or, at the very least, not ones identified by al-Khalīl.

What is interesting here is the realization that many Lebanese *zajal* metres cannot be reduced to strict Khalīlian metres, that some metres may not resemble Khalīlian metres at all, and that al-Ḥūrānī allows in his scansion the distinction between long and extra-long syllables which is not the most usual method in scanning *fuṣḥā* metres. All this will be discussed further.

Influenced by al-Ḥūrānī, whom he cites, Jurjī Zaydān states more emphatically that "the vernacular metres which have no counterpart in *fuṣḥā* metres are most probably taken from Syriac metrics."[35] This view has several proponents, such as Mārūn ʿAbbūd[36] and Anīs Frayḥa[37] who sees *qarrādī*, in particular, as a development from a Syriac seven-syllable metre used exclusively in church services by the early Maronite church fathers, first in Syriac, then in Karshūnī[38] and then in Arabic. Voicing a similar opinion, Tawfīq ʿAwwād, in a frequently quoted essay entitled 'al-Shiʿr al-ʿāmmī', sees all of *maʿannā* as scanning according to the *sarīʿ*, *rajaz*, and *wāfir* metres, excluding *qarrādī* which he believes has unlimited metres that vary with the various forms of

[34] Al-Ḥūrānī 1906, 604. Again, the statement is mere conjecture.

[35] Zaydān 1957, IV:207.

[36] See ʿAbbūd 1968, 68–73.

[37] Frayḥa 1973, 173, entry for *qarrādī*.

[38] Karshūnī refers to Arabic written in Syriac characters.

the genre. The most unusual *qarrādī*, he observes, consists of two feet, *maf'ūlātun / maf'ūlun* (_ _ _ _ / _ _ _), whose combination has not been recorded by al-Khalīl. ʿAwwād leaves the strong impression that the metre of *qarrādī* is a quantitative metre similar to but not known in Arabic metrics. He does not see a role for Syriac metrics in *zajal* poetry, although he does briefly mention the influence of Syriac church music on unspecified metres. As far as I have been able to ascertain from my own research, Syriac metrics is cited by writers with reference to *qarrādī* only, and this is not necessarily an inaccurate statement if *qarrādī* is used to refer to a particular metre in a syllabic-accentual system.[39]

The existence of two metrical systems in Lebanese *zajal* is suggested by Jean Lecerf in his important 'Littérature dialectale et renaissance arabe moderne',[40] a lengthy historical bibliography survey which also devotes several pages to the genres and metres of Lebanese *zajal*. Lecerf distinguishes two genres: 'les genres chantés' and 'les genres dits', listing under the former the *mawwāl*, *ʿatābā*, *mījanā*, *dalʿūnā*, and *shurūqī*, and under the latter *qaṣīd*, *maṭlaʿ* (*maʿannā*), *qarrādī*, and *jannāz*,[41] with a short

[39] One possible exception is Anīs Frayḥa's unsubstantial claim that "the poetic metres that they, the Lebanese, use to compose verses of *mījanā* and *maʿannā* are Syriac in origin, based upon the syllable." This is all that Frayḥa says before he refers the reader to Whaybeh 1952. See Frayḥa 1957, 274.

[40] Lecerf 1932, 239.

[41] Lecerf 1932, 234–37.

definition of each of them.[42] Only *qarrādī* is described metrically. "It is composed of seven long syllables in principle but may admit a supplementary short syllable which does not count in the measure."[43] As for the metrical systems of *zajal,* Lecerf has the following to say, despite, as he puts it, "the difficulties of the subject:"[44]

> Le point le plus original de la prosodie libanaise est l'existence apparente de deux systèmes aussi différents que le vers 'mesuré' (*mawzūn*), dont le rythme repose sur la quantité des syllabes, et le vers à nombre fixe de syllabes. Nous avons dit que ce dernier rythme est celui du *qarrādī*. Le problème qui se pose est d'abord de celui de la réalité de ce double système. En second lieu vient celui de son origine, et de lo possibilité d'une influence de la poésie syriaque. Il est très remarquable en effet que le vers 'nombré' (non-mesuré), de sept syllabes soit précisément celui des hymnes de Ephrem.

> (The most original aspect of Lebanese prosody is the apparent existence of two systems as different as measured verse [*mawzūn*], whose rhythm is based on the quantity of syllables, and verse with a fixed number of syllables. We have stated that this latter rhythm is that of the *qarrādī*. The first problem that arises is the reality of this dual system. Secondly, there is the question of its origin and the possibility of an influence from Syriac poetry. It is indeed very remarkable that the 'numbered' [non-measured]

[42] The definitions leave out questions of meters and concentrate instead on rhyme schemes and a brief account of content.

[43] Lecerf 1932, 237.

[44] Lecerf 1932, 239.

verse of seven syllables is precisely that of the hymns of Ephrem.)

Lecerf identifies 'le vers mesuré' with *maʿannā*, citing the aforementioned statements of al-Ḥūrānī, Zaydān, and ʿAwwād, among others, as clear indication of the workings of a quantitative system. He himself does not offer any examples, although he senses that "le principe paraît indiscutable" ("the principle seems indisputable")[45] and that despite the difficulty of scanning, as soon as the quantity of syllables enters the picture, one must end up with something resembling the metrics of al-Khalīl. The second system, "le vers à nombre fixe de syllabes," is that of *qarrādī* which Lecerf insists is composed of seven syllables and resembles the verse used in the hymns of Saint Ephrem. The question that poses itself here is: Is *qarrādī* the only metre in this system? If it is, then it contradicts the available data on *zajal* where poems of four, five, six, seven, eight or more syllables are found. If, on the other hand, *qarrādī* is the general name of a syllabic system composed of more than one metre, then Lecerf does not mention these. It is remarkable that Lecerf cites an old *qarrādiyya* which, according to his own reading, consists of an unequal number of syllables, but he blames such inconsistency on incertitude in the pronunciation of the lines. He also cites example of *dalʿūnā*[46] to which other critics attribute a five-syllable scansion,[47] but he neither clearly treats it as part of his second system nor indicates whether it is quantitatively scanned. Interestingly enough, he does not

[45] Lecerf 1932, 237.

[46] Lecerf 1932, 245.

[47] Lecerf 1932, 245.

mention the possible role of accent in his citing of Dalmann,[48] though he leaves his position unclear, and opts instead for number of syllables as the most important formal characteristic of *qarrādī*. Also citing Littmann,[49] Lecerf seems to agree that music plays a role in *qarrādī*, but he leaves it at that. Insightful as Lecerf's remarks are, the metre of *qarrādī* will be shown in its various manifestations to be determined by a stress pattern imposed upon it by a pattern of musical beats which explain the apparent fluctuation in number of syllables. Finally, to demonstrate the likelihood that *qarrādī* is a syllabic rather than a quantitative metre (the quantitative structure of *khabab*, for example), Lecerf appeals to the characteristics of the Lebanese dialect with its preponderant use of long syllables in the manner of Syriac.[50] He considers the possibility of a direct influence from examples cited by Ibn Khaldūn, which would suggest an Arabic metrical parentage, but he argues against a prototypical quantitative basis on the grounds that these examples "paraît bien aventuré, mais possible à la rigueur" ("seem quite adventurous, but possible if necessary").[51]

There is no question that Lecerf has touched on the problems involved in scanning *zajal*, that he has been conscious of dialectical problems, and that he has observed the presence of two metrical systems, but, by and large, his study rests on the

---

[48] The reference is to Dalmann 1901. See Lecerf 1932, 240.

[49] The reference is to Littmann 1902. See Lecerf 1932, 240.

[50] Lecerf 1932, 239–42.

[51] Lecerf 1932, 242.

authority of preceding critics and on impressions rarely supported by metrical analysis. He is more concerned with the forms of *zajal*, its history, development and content.

More comprehensive and perhaps problematic is Munīr Whaybeh's *al-Zajal: tārīkhuhu, adabuhu, aʿlāmuhu qadīman wa-ḥadīthan* (*The* Zajal*: Its History, Literature and Main Figures, Past and Present*) which, since its publication in 1952, has become a highly quoted source of *zajal* metrics. It is more comprehensive because it claims to be the most thorough discussion in Arabic of *zajal* metres, containing a large number of representative poems spanning the period from the earliest recorded *zajal*s until the present. It is more problematic because it posits a simple syllabic basis for these metres, which appears convincing at first but then collapses under scrutiny and careful reference to existing data. Whaybeh is categorical about the number of metres, thirteen in all, that obtain in *zajal*. The number is significant, for it is the same that scholarship attributes to Syriac metres,[52] which, to say the least, is a curious coincidence. His nomenclature is entirely new in that it is taken, as he claims, from a study by a Syriac Monophysite monk Anṭūn al-Tikrītī who lived in the ninth century. This is confusing because the author does not indicate whether al-Tikrītī's study deals with Syriac poetry or with Lebanese *zajal*. It is, we are told, a study detailing the rules of composition, *qawāʿid al-naẓm*, but he chooses illustrations from modern written *zajal*, rather than examples from the ninth century, or modern oral recitation. The problem is that no one else besides

[52] See, for example, Burgess 1853, p. lix.

Whaybeh has written about these metres. When asked about the metres of *zajal*, poets and critics alike refer to Whaybeh's thirteen metres, but when pressed they can hardly identify five or six of them and then always using the nomenclature of al-Khalīl's metres. What this means is that either more than half of the thirteen metres are no longer used, or that they have assumed new names. Be that as it may, Whaybeh's classifications represent a challenge with which this study must deal.

Drawing upon his source, Whaybeh states that the early poets "used in their poetry two kinds of compositions, *ḍarbān min al-naẓm*: *al-mutawāzī* (i.e., regular, mono-metric) and *al-mukhtalif* (i.e., metrically mixed), the former consisting of two hemistichs, *daʿāmatayn* or one verse unit,[53] *daʿāma wāḥida*, while the latter appearing in different *daʿāʾim* and irregular number of syllables, or *ḥarakāt*, in the various lines of the poem."[54] *Al-mutawāzī*, moreover, has thirteen metres whose *awzān* ('rhythmic patterns', one would assume) "are limitless and hard to manage, as is the case today with *maʿannā* and its derivations."[55] What all this means is not very clear, for Whaybeh often uses the terms *baḥr* ('metre'), *naẓm* ('composition') and *wazn* ('rhythm') interchangeably, confusing metre with rhythm and musical style. The second kind of *naẓm*, for example, has, according to Whaybeh, "various *taqāsīm* ('musical arrangements'?) and rhythmic patterns (*awzān*)

---

[53] Whaybeh 1952, 32.

[54] Whaybeh 1952, 32.

[55] Whaybeh 1952, 32.

numbering more than one hundred and sixty-five."[56] Quoting from a manuscript entitled *Bijkāz al-shaykh*, found, according to him, in a monastery in Kisirwān (Lebanon)[57] Whaybeh then lists nineteen *awzān* which turn out to be various names for church litanies and musical scores, rather than metres. Although he implies that there seems to be a relationship between metre and hymnology, he does not explore the matter further.

At this point, his discussion of the *mutawāzī*'s thirteen metres is more relevant. These metres are listed as follows according to the number of syllables in the hemistich or the verse unit:[58]

Name of Metre	Number of Hemistichs	Number of Syllables	Syllable Number in First Hemistich	Syllable Number in Second Hemistich
al-aswānī	2	6	3	3
al-mutasāwī	2	8	4	4
al-mutawaṣṣiṭ	2	10	5	5
al-mutaqārib	2	12	6	6
al-muzdawij	2	14	7	7
al-mutafāwit	2	16	8	8
al-mutanāhī	2	18	9	9
al-sarīʿ	2	20	10	10
al-basīṭ	2	22	11	11
al-yaʿqūbī	2	24	12	12
al-wafāʾī	1	13	13	–
al-mutawāzī	1	14	14	–
al-kāmil	1	15	15	–

[56] Whaybeh 1952, 41.

[57] Whaybeh 1952, 41.

[58] Whaybeh 1952, 33.

This mechanical classification does not account for the difference between short, long, or extra-long syllables, and the four metres—*al-mutaqārib*, *al-sarīʿ*, *al-basīṭ*, and *al-kāmil*—do not bear any resemblance to their counterparts in al-Khalīl's system. The last three metres—*al-wafāʾī*, *al-mutawāzī*, and *al-kāmil*—are in verse units. The maximum number of syllables in a verse unit is fifteen, and in a two-hemistich verse, twenty-four. This, in brief, is a syllabic metrical description which does not provide for quality or quantity of syllable. If stress is at all operative in this system, it is not mentioned, unless by *wazn* the author means a particular rhythmic pattern with accompanying stress. At any rate, the examples cited in his study are little more than indiscriminate counting of syllables. Two bewildering statements complicate the issue further. First, we are told:

> All the metrical units (or *tafāʿīl*) in all the metres can be formed or taken from the well-known feet of *fuṣḥā* poetry, on condition attention is paid to the number of syllables (or *ḥarakāt*) in the particular line and the number of syllables in each hemistich (i.e., when the line is composed of two hemistichs). It is acceptable when composing vernacular poetry to vowel a quiescent consonant and to remove the vowel of a vowelled consonant without any limitation or condition (*bidūn qayd wa-lā sharṭ*).[59]

How, on the one hand, we can derive the metrical units or feet of *zajal* metres from the quantitative system of *fuṣḥā* poetry and at the same time make no allowance for fluctuation in the number and quantity of syllables is not clear. If it is indeed the case

[59] Whaybeh 1952, 33.

that the feet can be derived from those of *fuṣḥā,* then it makes better sense to argue for some kind of quantitative basis for *zajal.* Add to this the untenable assertion that vowels can be displaced with no deference to meaning, and Whaybeh's statement becomes harder to accept. The dislocation of vowels must be pegged, it seems to me, to the morphology of words in the dialect which impose limitation on the way lines are rendered.

On the other hand, Whaybeh's basic rule for scansion suggests that quantity does play a role, although such a role is not properly assessed or analysed in the examples he cites. "[T]he rhythmic unit (*waḥdat al-wazn*)," he states, "is achieved by giving every letter pronounced in speech its equal time value to letters similar to it."[60] In other words, short and long syllables are delimited by an abstract time factor that distinguishes them quantitatively in much the same way as scansion of *fuṣḥā* is produced. Yet Whaybeh's examples are quite inconsistent in this respect. "A quiescent consonant," he adds, "comprises part of the letter (or syllable) that precedes it."[61] Again, this rule is not always followed in the scansion that he attempts. Whaybeh, for example, illustrates his scansion method for a two-hemistich *mutaqārib* line which, according to his system, breaks into twelve syllables.

Min hal jabal bihdīk // *Rīḥān wi-ghnānī*[62]
'From this mountain I give you as a present' // 'Basil and songs'

The following syllabic picture emerges:

[60] Whaybeh 1952, 34.

[61] Whaybeh 1952, 34.

[62] Whaybeh 1952, 35.

Min	*hal*	*jab*	*al*	*bih*	*dīk*	//	*Rī*	*ḥā*	*n*	*wigh*	*nā*	*nī*
1	2	3	4	5	6		1	2	3	4	5	6

What is overlooked here is the presence of a short third syllable in each hemistich, which will yield the familiar *fuṣḥā* quantitative configuration: _ _ ᴗ _ / _ $\__{o}$ // _ _ ᴗ _ / _ _, with an extra-long syllable at the end of the first hemistich. If it is simply a question of syllable number, then why is it that every one of the eight lines of the *mutaqārib* cited has a short third syllable in every hemistich?[63] Also, following Whaybeh's classification, one hemistich of *al-aswānī* when joined with one hemistich of *al-mutasāwī* will yield theoretically a hemistich of *al-muzdawij* since stress and syllable length do not seem to count. But such a combination does not work even when we take full advantage of vowel displacement. Consider Whaybeh's scansion of *al-aswānī* and *al-mutasāwī*:

Al-aswānī

Nha	*ziw*	*mād*	//	*Rik*	*nil*	*ṣadr*[64]
1	2	3		1	2	3
[N]haz	*ziw*	*mād*	//	*Rik*	*niṣ*	*ṣadr*[65]

'The chest's foundations have been shaken'

Al-mutasāwī

Lib	*nān*	*mash*	*hūr*	//	*Bay*	*nil*	*bil*	*dān*
1	2	3	4		1	2	3	4

'Lebanon is famous' // 'Among the countries'

---

[63] Whaybeh 1952, 35.

[64] Whaybeh 1952, 34.

[65] Compare Whaybeh's arbitrary syllabic division: *nhaz* instead of *[n]haz*, *zziw* rather than *ziw*, and the scansion goes against Arabic morphology.

Theoretically, *Nhaz-ziw mād Libnān mashhūr* would give us

Ḍay	*ʿit*	*nā*	*maf*	*rū*	*shī*	*zhūr*
1	2	3	4	5	6	7

(more correctly, *Ḍay ʿit nā maf rū shiz hūr*, 'Our village is blanketed with flowers'), which Whaybeh gives as an example of a *muzdawij* hemistich.[66]

Overlooking for a moment Whaybeh's curious division of syllables, the line *[N]haz ziw mād Libnān mashhūr* and the *muzdawij* hemistich *Ḍayʿitnā mafrūshi zhūr* do not have the same rhythm when read by a Lebanese. The reasons are manifold, but the most important one is that all three metres have a basic stress pattern, which, when tampered with, produces a different rhythmic effect.

There is no room here to go into details about the stress patterns of *zajal* metres. This is reserved for a later stage in this analysis. It is important, however, to note that even when the combination of *al-aswānī* and *al-mutasāwī* yields a pattern of stress similar to one of *al-muzdawij*'s pattern, the line will still not yield the rhythm of *al-muzdawij*. One important reason is the length of the syllables involved. In the *al-muzdawij* example cited above, the first six syllables are long and the seventh is extra-long. In the theoretical example, *[N]haz-ziw mād Libnān mashhūr*, syllables three, five and seven are all extra-long, which imposes an impossible effort upon the reader or the singer to approximate the rhythmic pattern of *al-muzdawij*. If it can be done at all, a consequent slurring of syllables takes place and the line sounds

66 Whaybeh 1952, 36.

nonsensical to the listener. To put it differently, the line will have to be read as follows:

[N]haz-ziw mad Lib nan mash hūr

— — — — — — —o

instead of

[N]haz-ziw mād Lib nān mash hūr

— — —o — —o — —o

with the unavoidable consequence of destroying the meanings of the words, *mād* and *Libnān*. It is important to note in this respect that the following anonymous line will fall in Whaybeh's classification under *al-mutasāwī* metre:

Shū hal ʾiṣṣa //	*Ma lha nhāyeh*
— — — —	— — — —
'What tale this is! //	It has no ending'

but which when read aloud will have a different rhythm altogether from *Libnān mashūr bayn il-bildān*, the line with which Whaybeh illustrates the scansion of *al-mutasāwī*.

Whaybeh might object that combining one hemistich from one metre with that of another metre is not acceptable and that division into hemistichs and verse units is an important distinctive feature of his metrical system. Even if we grant that his discussion of his system implies this caution, still it fails to explain why in practice *zajal* poems contain lines of unequal number of syllables and particular alternations of short, long, and extra-long syllables. The following two-hemistich lines delivered orally by

Zaghlūl al-Dāmūr[67] will illustrate the difference between theory and practice:

[L]-in	*sān*	*[i]*	*law*	*mā*	*ki*	*lim*	*tub*	*tin*	*ʾāl*	//
—	—	ᴗ	—	—	ᴗ	—	—	—	—o	
1	2	3	4	5	6	7	8	9	10	

'If man did not have the power of speech'

Kān	*[i]*	*al*	*lāh*	*byikh*	*la*	*ʾū*	*tim*	*thāl*[68]
—	ᴗ	—	—o	—	ᴗ	—	—	—o
1	2	3	4	5	6	7	8	9

'God would have created him a statue'

The final extra-long syllable in each hemistich notwithstanding, the number of syllables is ten in the first and nine in the second. There are two short syllables in each, and number six in both is a short one.[69] These are all important features that the non-discriminating syllabic-scansion method cannot explain.

Over and above such limitations there remains the problem of Whaybeh's inconsistent scansion practice. His assertion that a

---

[67] The line is taken from a taped interview with Zaghlūl during which the author of this work asked the poet to give illustrations on all the *zajal* meters that the poet knew.

[68] Syllables 6 and 7 in both hemistichs can be easily transposed without affecting the rhythm. *Kilimtū* could also be read as *kilmitū*; likewise, *[b]yikhlaʾū* could be rendered *[b]yikhilʾū*, thus causing the transposition. The extra-long syllable 4 in hemistich 2 could change to a long one if a liaison between it and 5 is made. At any rate, the short syllables in these hemistichs are important formal features, whether they are 6 or 7 in the hemistich.

[69] Clearly the syllabic system is not concerned with the quantitative difference between syllables.

quiescent consonant is to be considered part of the syllable preceding it does not seem true with reference to several of his examples. On the one hand, for example, he scans *Rīḥān wi-ghnānī* into *Rī ḥā n wigh nā nī*, or a total of six syllables, giving the quiescent consonant *n* the value of one syllable. On the other hand, in *Libnān mashhūr*, he produces four syllables (*Lib*, *nān*, *mash*, *hūr*), this time choosing not to give the *n* in *Libnān* any value at all. Similarly, in his illustration of *al-wafāʾī* metre he scans *Lā tnām ʿa ḍ-ḍaym la tishki l-dahir law jār* as follows:

Lā	*tnā*	*m*	*ʿa*	*lā*	*ḍaym*	*lā*	*tish*	*kid*	*da*	*hir*	*law*	*jār*[70]
1	2	3	4	5	6	7	8	9	10	11	12	13

'Don't sleep on a wrong;
don't rail against fate when it bears down on you'

breaking *ʿaḍḍaym* into *ʿa lā daym*, which does not seem necessary for syllable count in the line as a whole, and making *tnām* yield two syllables, *tnā* and *m*. As to why the *mīm* in *ʿaḍḍaym* is not part of the syllabic division is not clear, especially since both *mīms* are pronounced in speech. What is clear, however, is that an extra-long syllable such as *tnām* or *ḍaym* is not always considered as two syllables, though Whaybeh neither treats the point nor seems to attach to it any value.

In the rest of his study the author attempts to distinguish some of the confusion surrounding metre and genre by discussing the genres of *zajal* and identifying the particular metres employed in them. Unfortunately, this method ends, at times, by exacerbating the problem. The two main genres that emerge are

[70] Whaybeh 1952, 38.

*al-ma*ʿ*annā* and *al-qarrādī*, each with numerous *anwā*ʿ ('kinds'). To these are added three main *ṭarā*ʾ*iq*: *al-ḥidā*, *al-zalghaṭa* or *al-zaghrada*, and *al-nadb*, along with what he terms "*aghānī lubnāniyya ḥadītha*" ('modern Lebanese songs') such as *abū al-zuluf*, *al-*ʿ*atābā*, *al-mījanā*, *al-shurūqī* or *al-qaṣīd al-badawī*, and *al-mawwāl al-baghdādī*, in much the same vein as Nakhleh's classifications.[71] While most of his discussion of *al-ma*ʿ*annā* and its kinds centres around descriptions of stanza forms and rhyme schemes, he does identify mainly three of his metres (*al-ya*ʿ*qūbī*, *al-sarī*ʿ, *al-mutaqārib*) and one example of *al-muzdawij* which he does not name. Most of the *ma*ʿ*annā* 'genres'[72] seem to employ *al-ya*ʿ*qūbī* and *al-sarī*ʿ, that is, metres of twelve and eleven syllables respectively, to use his syllabic classification. The example of *al-mutaqārib* that he cites is taken from a poem in *al-sarī*ʿ metre by Rashīd Nakhleh in which only the *kharjas* are in the *mutaqārib*.[73] Again, one of the examples cited shows a combination of *al-aswānī* with a two-hemistich metre composed of eleven syllables per hemistich, which Whaybeh's classification does not account for and which, therefore, is not named at all. But here, once more, the poem is from Rashīd Nakhleh's book and bears no resemblance to oral *zajal* compositions. On the other hand, the verses used to illustrate *al-qaṣīd al-mujazzam*, one of the kinds (*anwā*ʿ) of *ma*ʿ*annā* according to Whaybeh, employ a two-hemistich fourteen-syllable metre in one instance and a twelve-syllable two-

---

[71] Whaybeh 1952, 63–70.

[72] Whaybeh 1952, 66–67.

[73] Whaybeh 1952, 67.

hemistich metre in the other.[74] On the first metre Whaybeh cites the following couplet:

خْصاني جالِ بْسوق إِمجال // وْهَزِّ رْجال عْلى الْمَيْلَيْن

Ḥṣānī jāl b-sūʾ ʾimjāl // W-hazz [i]rjāl[i] ʿla l-maylayn

[Ḥ]ṣā nī jā l[i]b- sūʾ ʾim jāl // [W-] haz zir jā liʿ lal- may layn

— — — — — — — // — — — — — — — —

'My horse moved freely in a wide field' //

'And shook up the men on both sides'

خَصمي زال وْدَمعي سال // وْعَنّي مال بْلَمحِة عَين

Khaṣmī zāl w-damʿī sāl // W-ʿannī māl b-lamḥit ʿayn

Khaṣ mī zā l[i]w- dam ʿī sāl // [w-]ʿan nī mā l[i]b- lam ḥit ʿayn

— — — — — — — // — — — — — — —

'My enemy vanished, and my tears flowed' //

'And away from me he went in a trice'

Now if the couplet is divided into smaller metrical units,

[Ḥ]ṣānī jāl // *[b]-sūʾ ʾimjāl*

— — — // — — —

[W-]hazz [i]rjāl // [ʿ]la l-maylayn

— — — // — — —

Khaṣmī zāl // *[w]-damʿī sāl*

— — — // — — —

[W-]ʿannī māl // *[b]-lamḥit ʿayn*

— — — // — — —

it will yield three lines of Whaybeh's *al-aswānī* metre, because the seventh syllable in the first configuration, obtained from the *waṣl* between the extra-long syllables and the ensuing quiescent consonants, will be dropped at rest position at hemistich end. I

[74] Whaybeh 1952, 71–76.

mention this example in particular because it throws further doubt on Whaybeh's metrical classification. Is this an illustration of *al-aswānī* or *al-muzdawij* metre? Whaybeh does not supply us with the answer. His second example of *al-qaṣīd al-mujazzam* bears no metrical semblance to the first:

> *Mā zāl[i] ḥubb il-ghayr[i] fī ʿaynik ḥilī* //
> — — ᴗ — — — ᴗ — — — ᴗ —//
> 'Since loving others has become appealing to your eyes' //
> *Ṣār[i] wājib waddiʿik fī-mā yalī*
> — ᴗ — — — ᴗ — — — ᴗ —
> 'It is important to bid you farewell with what follows'

which Whaybeh would scan,

Mā	*zā*	*l*	*ḥib*	*bil*	*ghay*	*r*	*fī*	*ʾay*	*nik*	*ḥi*	*lī*
1	2	3	4	5	6	7	8	9	10	11	12
Ṣā	*r*	*wā*	*jib*	*wad*	*di*	*ʿik*	*fī*	*mā*	*ya*	*lī*	
1	2	3	4	5	6	7	8	9	10	11	

Not only are short vowels important features of these two hemistichs (the previous example consisted of long vowels only), but here there is also a discrepancy in the number of syllables between one and the other. At first sight it appears Whaybeh is saying that *al-qaṣīd al-mujazzam* employs two different metres, but it is more likely that he is defining the word *mujazzam* rather than *qaṣīd*, a rhyme scheme, perhaps a verse form, rather than a metrical pattern. Whaybeh seems to have read the first example with strong caesural stops, a forced reading which recitation of singing does not allow.

According to Whaybeh, one kind of *maʿannā* is *al-muwashshaḥ*, a strophic form resembling one of the many manifestations of the Andalusian prototype, whose metre is a combination of *al-muzdawij* (seven syllables) and *al-mutasāwī* (four syllables):

> *ʿAm tiḍḥak bi-l-bindayrah //* *Arzit Libnān*
>
> — — — — — — — // — — — —o
>
> 'Laughing joyfully on the flag //
> is the Cedar of Lebanon'
>
> *[W]-rāʿi [b]-laḥn il-minjayrah //* *[Y]hizz il-widyān*
>
> — — — — — — — — // — — — —o
>
> 'And a shepherd with the tunes of the flute //
> is shaking the valleys'

yet another example taken from Rashīd Nakhleh shows a completely different metre for *al-maʿannā al-muwashshaḥ*. This time it is a *mutaqārib*, though Whaybeh is not specific:

> *[M]ni shar[ʾi] yā ḥādī //* *ʿArrij ʿala l-wādī*
>
> — — ᴗ — — —// — — ᴗ — — —
>
> 'From the East, O, *ḥādī* ('singer of *ḥidā*') // 'Pass by the valley'

Emerging from all this is that *al-maʿannā* is not associated with any one metre, rather a strophic form in several metres. While this may be largely true, the term *maʿannā* seems to have acquired with Whaybeh a wide significance subsuming most of *zajal*. Perhaps his reliance in his examples on Rashīd Nakhleh's book, *Maʿannā Rashīd Nakhleh*, which, despite the prominence it gives in the title to *maʿannā*, also contains numerous examples of *qarrādī*, *ʿatābā*, *mījanā*, and other genres, made him expand *maʿannā* to many more metres than other critics and poets allow. While *maʿannā* is used sometimes interchangeably with *zajal*, it is also specifically used by the poets interviewed for this study to refer to one poetic metre only. For example, Joseph al-Hāshim, better known as Zaghlūl al-Dāmūr ('the singing dove of Dāmūr'), clearly considers *al-maʿannā* as belonging to a particular metre without limiting that metre to *maʿannā* as genre only. Whaybeh, of course, does not distinguish between *maʿannā* and *qaṣīd*. The latter he treats as part of the many forms of the former.

Turning then to *qarrādī*, Whaybeh discusses eight forms, six of which employ *al-muzdawij* metre and two *al-basīṭ* and *al-sarīʿ*. He is alone among critics in admitting more than one metre for *qarrādī*, though ʿAwwād speaks of unlimited metres as we have seen above. It is most likely that his examples on *al-basīṭ* and *al-sarīʿ* have nothing to do with *qarrādī* at all and that he is once more unsure of the distinction between metre and form. One of the examples he cites on *al-qarrādī al-muwashshaḥ* could very well belong to *al-maʿannā* since scansion reveals that it is none other than *al-maʿannā al-muwashshaḥ*. Why the one is *maʿannā* and the other is *qarrādī* is left unexplained. The second example taken from a poem by al-Shaykh Nāṣīf al-Yāzijī (1800–1871) who, according to Whaybeh, "invented" this metre[75] appears to scan into ten syllables per hemistich, with the third and seventh syllables being short throughout the poem. Among the critics only Whaybeh identifies it as *qarrādī*. When it comes to *ṭarāʾiq al-zajal* and *al-aghānī*, Whaybeh's breakdown of genres and metres appears as follows:

Genre	Metre
al-ḥidā and *al-nadb*	*al-mutafāwit*
al-zalghaṭa	*al-basīṭ*
al-ʿatābā	*al-sarīʿ*

[75] Whaybeh 1952, 74.

al-mījanā	*al-yaʿqūbī*
abū al-zuluf and *al-shurūqī*	*al-wafāʾī*
al-mawwāl al-baghdādī	*al-mutawāzī*

All in all, we have a very confusing account of metres and genres, not unlike that of the critics who preceded the author in time. Most of the examples, it seems to me, are tailored to fit Whaybeh's scansion rules and to satisfy his metrical system. Above, I questioned many of Whaybeh's scansion methods and metrical analyses. Now, in light of the available research on Syriac poetry, I am convinced that Whaybeh assumes that the metres of Lebanese *zajal* are no different from those which writers on Syriac poetry attribute to that poetry. Curiously enough, the number of Syriac metres most widely accepted by Syriac scholars is thirteen, which is the same number that Whaybeh categorically assigns to Lebanese *zajal*.[76] Quoting Stephen, a Maronite Patriarch who had written a treatise on the tunes of the Syrians, Benedict, one of the earliest translators of Saint Ephrem, says that Stephen reduces these tunes to six classes:

> The first… consists of verses of two metres, (*versibus bimetris*); the second, of verses of three metres, (and so on until we come to the sixth); but the sixth class varies, and is formed of both simple and compound numbers. He [Stephen] afterwards reduces the whole Syriac poetry to certain titles, as it were kinds of songs…, and then numbers them as they were presented to him in ancient manuscripts. They are thirteen in number, and all are alike in that they follow a certain metrical law, but they differ in

[76] Whaybeh 1952, 33.

> modulation, and some also in their subject matter [*argumento*].[77]

Probing then the meaning of *versibus bimetris* and *trimetris*, etc., Henry Burgess suggests that these pertain to poems consisting "of verses of two different measures, as penta-syllabic and hepta-syllabic alternately; and so of the rest."[78] This is precisely what Whaybeh means by *al-jawāzāt fī al-shiʿr al-ʿāmmī* (the licences of vernacular poetry).[79] In brief, Whaybeh is in fact talking about Syriac poetry which may share a great number of features with Lebanese *zajal*, but which also cannot explain an equally great number of features characteristic of Lebanese poetry alone. Denying, as Whaybeh does, any basis for the operation of a quantitative system in *zajal* does not seem to accord with the reality of this poetry today. A careful study of his scansion reveals without doubt that several of his metres consist of well-defined feet, in most cases not different at all from the feet of *fuṣḥā* poetry. Other critics hold tenaciously to a quantitative basis for *zajal*.

In 1966 Jabbour Abdel-Nour (Jabbūr ʿAbd al-Nūr) published *Études sur la poésie dialectale au Liban* (*Studies on the Vernacular Poetry of Lebanon*), the only book-length study of Lebanese *zajal* in French. The book is cited by Whaybeh in 1952 as a forthcoming study in French entitled *al-Shiʿr wa-al-lugha al-ʿāmmiyya* (*Poetry and Vernacular Language*).[80] Which book was finished first is not a matter of great importance, but what is

---

[77] Burgess 1853, 59.

[78] Burgess 1853, 60.

[79] Whaybeh 1952, 39.

[80] Whaybeh 1952, 27.

significant is that Abdel-Nour chose to leave Whaybeh's book out of his list of references despite the fact that Whaybeh's book appeared fourteen years before his own. Undoubtedly, the reason lies in the two authors' entirely different interpretations of the metrics of *zajal*, and in Abdel-Nour's reluctance to consider the workings of a syllabic system. In no equivocal terms he states:

> En tenant compte de l'inexactitude de la notation selon l'orthographe classique, de l'instabilité phonétique d'un grand nombre de mots, des licences prosodiques, des chutes internes des voyelles, et du son (i) de jonction, nous pouvons conclure que la metrique du zajal est fondée sur la quantité. Comme nous le constaterons un peu plus loin, en étudiant les différents groupements de vers, cette métrique concord eaves [sic.] certains metres classiques (arabes).
>
> (Taking into account the inaccuracy of notation according to classical orthography, the phonetic instability of a large number of words, prosodic licences, the internal elision of vowels, and the junction sound [i], we can conclude that the metre of *zajal* is based on quantity. As we will see a little further on, in studying the different groupings of verses, this metre aligns with certain classical [Arabic] metres.)[81]

While it is true that certain considerations have to be taken into account in the scansion of *zajal*, it does not follow necessarily that all *zajal* metres scan quantitatively. Abdel-Nour's illustrations or metrical patterns are not always documented. We are told, for example, that *al-shurūqī* scans according to the *basīṭ*

[81] Abdel-Nour 1957, 97.

metre of al-Khalīl without supporting evidence,[82] that *dalʿūnā* (or *dalʿonā*)[83] scans quantitatively as _ _ / _ _ _, without supplying us with the reason for the division into two and three syllables[84] (instead, for example, of three and two or two, two, and one), that "another genre" of *ḥidā* is composed after *rajaz*, again without proof, that *ḥidā* "generally" breaks into the following quantitative pattern: _ _ _ / _ _ _ / _ _ _,[85] and that both *dalʿūnā* and "a variety" of *ḥidā* are derivatives of *qarrādī*,[86] which, one assumes, is due to the appearance in them of only long syllables.

Reserving the term *zajal* for all Lebanese vernacular poetry, Abdel-Nour identifies eleven "genres" and six basic quantitative metres. He sums up his metrical analysis as follows:

a) The *rajaz*, in the *maʿannā*, the *mījanā* and one genre of *ḥidā*;
b) The *basīṭ*, in the *shurūqī*, the *mawwāl*, the *zalāghīt*, *abū al-zuluf*, and the *maʿannā*;
c) The *wāfir*, in the *maʿannā* and the *ʿatābā*;
d) The *ramal*, in the *nadb*;
e) At times the *sarīʿ* in the *maʿannā*;

---

[82] Abdel-Nour 1957, 102–4.

[83] Abdel-Nour 1957, 106.

[84] Abdel-Nour 1957, 106.

[85] Abdel-Nour 1957, 106.

[86] Abdel-Nour 1957, 106.

f) The derivation of *qarrādī, dalʿūnā* and a variety of *ḥidā* from the *khabab* metre should be added with some reservations.[87]

It should be noted here that Abdel-Nour does not attempt to discuss the licences that these metres manifest in their adaptation to *zajal* poetry. Whatever licences are taken, he implies, are those that al-Khalīl's system allows. The curious absence of the *qaṣīd* from the eleven genres he enumerates should also be noted. He does not seem to distinguish between *maʿannā* and *qaṣīd*, which may explain, in part, why he assumes that *maʿannā* appears in *rajaz, basīṭ, wāfir,* and *sarīʿ*.

The *qarrādī* presents the main problem for Abdel-Nour and, as we have seen, to most of the critics before him. "Beaucoup d'éléments," he writes, "font croire que le *qarrādī* échappe au principe général des mètres quantitatifs adoptés en dialecte."[88] ("Many elements suggest that the *qarrādī* escapes the general principle of quantitative metres adopted in dialect.") These "éléments" are not enumerated, but one main reason emerges from Abdel-Nour's ensuing argument. Because the syllabic metres lend themselves, more than quantitative metres to "coupures, omissions et additions" ("cuts, omissions, and additions")[89] and because all the syllables in *qarrādī* are long,[90] it is most likely, he says, that we are dealing with a variety of *al-khabab* metre.

---

[87] Abdel-Nour 1957, 108.

[88] Abdel-Nour 1957, 100.

[89] Abdel-Nour 1957, 100.

[90] Abdel-Nour 1957, 100.

Although he does admit the frequent presence of short syllables in *qarrādī*, he dismisses their importance because, as he puts it, they are necessarily elongated "pour être assimilées aux longues" ("to be assimilated to long ones).[91] While my research seems to support Abdel-Nour's observation concerning the elongation of one or more short syllables, there is also the more important observation that *qarrādī* may contain more than seven syllables, be they long or short, and that such an occurrence will not affect the metre. The principle involved here concerns a pattern of stress which levels out the effect of uneven numbers of syllables, and a musical metre superimposed upon the poetic one. The possibility that *al-khabab* may be the metre of *qarrādī* notwithstanding, the reasons for that seem to be in the province of music not metrics. I shall return to this point later on.

Much of the criticism discussed above abounds in impressionistic statements, contradictions, shaky terminology and serious lack of documentation. The studies of Whaybeh and Abdel-Nour fail, I think, to justify their insistence on a syllabic system in the case of the former, or a quantitative system in the case of the latter. Whaybeh introduces the largest number of metres, several more than the six *fuṣḥā* metres identified by Abdel-Nour, unless Abdel-Nour considers metres resembling *al-aswānī* and *al-mutawāzī* shorter versions of *qarrādī*. None of the critics admits music, song, and stress into metrical study. All of them, with the exception of Whaybeh, single out *qarrādī* as the most problematic of all because the only Arabic metre which appears to resemble

---

[91] Abdel-Nour 1957, 100.

it is *al-khabab*, a metre not identified, or intentionally overlooked by al-Khalīl, though recognised by al-Akhfash (d. 793) and later critics as an indigenous Arabic metre.

3. *FUṢḤĀ* AND *ZAJAL* METRES

It is important at the outset to establish that some *zajal* metres may be derived with utmost ease from well-known *fuṣḥā* metres. Such proof serves at once to explain the probable origin of some *zajal* metres and, more significantly, explain the difficulty of scanning the earliest *zajals* in which *fuṣḥā* and dialect appear side by side. Consider the following line chosen from a poem in *fuṣḥā* by Būlus Salāma entitled *Min Lubnān* ('From Lebanon'):

> *Yā jibāla l-arzi yā ukhta s-samā* //
> 'Mountains of the Cedars, sisters of the skies' //
>
> *Ṭāba fīk il-mawtu baʿda l-ʿayshi ṭābā*
> 'Having enjoyed life in you, I look forward to dying there'

The scansion produces two hemistichs of the Khalīlian *ramal* metre whose ideal form is _ ᴗ _ _ / _ ᴗ _ _ / _ ᴗ _ _. In this example, however, the last foot of the first hemistich undergoes *iʿlāl*, specifically a *ḥadhf*[1] ('deletion of the last syllable of the foot') which shortens _ ᴗ _ _ to _ ᴗ _ throughout the poem.

Now, read straight as vernacular, the line yields the following syllabic breakdown:

> *Yā jbāl*[2] *il-arz ya ikht is-samā*
> _[ₒ] _ _ _ _ _ _ ᴗ _
> *Ṭāb fīk il-mawt baʿd il-ʿaysh ṭāb*
> _ₒ _ _ _ₒ _ _ _ₒ _ₒ

---

[1] In this instance *fāʿilātun* (_ ᴗ _ _) is shortened to *fāʿilun* (_ ᴗ _).

[2] Note the extra-long syllable *yāj* which contracts the vowel *i* in the *fuṣḥā* reading of *yā jibāl*.

https://doi.org/10.11647/OBP.0424.03

where characteristically most short syllables are lost. But declaimed or sung as a vernacular line of poetry, it yields two hemistichs resembling, with some modification, *al-ramal* metre:

> *Yā j[i]bāl il-ariz yā ikht is-samā*
>
> – ⏑ – – ⏑ – – – – ⏑ –
>
> *Ṭāb[i] fīk il-mawt[i] baʿd il-ʿaysh[i] ṭāb*
>
> – ⏑ – – – ⏑ – – – ⏑ –

or – ⏑ – – / –̆ ⏑̄ –̄ –̄ / – ⏑ – // – ⏑ – – / – ⏑ – – / – ⏑ –. The only difference is that the second hemistich loses the last syllable in the dialectical reading of *ṭābā* as *ṭāb*, and the second foot of the first hemistich reverts to (⏑ – – –) in one dialectical reading, but could in another reading produce (– ⏑ – –), depending on whether the Arabic word for 'cedar' is read as *ariz* or *arz*[*i*], both acceptable readings in dialect. There is no general rule for the metrical treatment of extra-long syllables. By and large, however, in most but not in all metres, a short vowel *i* is inserted after the extra-long syllable, or after the first consonant in some syllabic configurations, or just before the last consonant in others. Thus the following picture emerges:

1. *jār (CV̄C) jār[i]*
2. *qabr (CVCC) qabr[i]* or *qab[i]r*
3. *jbāl (CCV̄C) j[i]bāl*

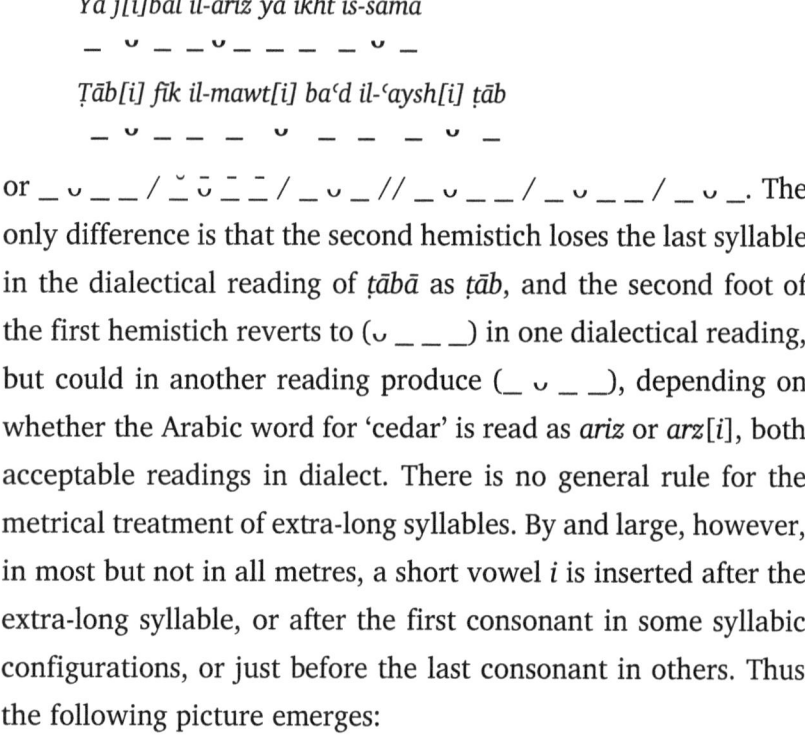

In all three instances, song, music, and oral delivery are the surest ways to determine where the vowel is inserted. At the end of the line, extra-long syllables are conventionally treated as long syllables except in the case of the ultra-long (e.g. *jbāl*) which is broken into a short and a long (⏑ —), *j[i]* and *bāl.*[3] It is to be noted that in some cases the poets may choose to pause after extra-long syllables rather than insert the vowel or they may simply reduce the quantity of an extra-long to a long. These are important observations which only music, song and oral delivery can explain, and of this more is to come.

The verse cited above shows that *al-ramal* of *fuṣḥā* can be easily adapted in *zajal*, and this points, I think, to an important formal characteristic shared by both *al-ramal* itself and the Lebanese dialect, namely that the dialectal suppression of the desinential and other terminal vowels does not substantially affect the rhythm of *al-ramal*. It also implies that other factors, such as stress, may be of much greater importance than quantity in determining rhythm, since the delivery of both the *fuṣḥā* and the vernacular versions of the line seem rhythmically compatible, with or without the insertion of the short vowels. I shall expand on this in the course of this study.

Consider now the following hemistich from another poem by Salāma:[4]

> *Lubnānu ḥiṣnu ḍ-ḍādi ṣā'inu ʿizzihā*
>
> — —⏑ — — —⏑ — ⏑⏑ —⏑ —
>
> 'Lebanon is the fortress of the Arabic language,
> protector of its glory'

---

[3] Cf. Abdel-Nour 1957, 96, where he argues for the addition of the short vowel *i*: "entre certains groupes consonantiques inarticulables," as he puts it.

[4] Salāma 1962, 135.

which consists of two feet of *al-rajaz* metre (_ _ ᴗ _) and one of *al-kāmil* (ᴗ ᴗ _ ᴗ _), and which traditional scansion would treat as a hemistich of *kāmil*[5] with a *ziḥāf* in the first two feet. When this hemistich was presented as a vernacular hemistich to several persons familiar with the Lebanese dialect, the readings, without exception, gave

Libnān hiṣni ḍ-ḍād ṣāyin ʿizzhā

— —o — — —o — — — —

which differs from the *fuṣḥā* scansion in that the short syllables are absent and that syllable number seven substitutes a long syllable to the two short ones of the *fuṣḥā* hemistich. Now when the same persons were asked to sing it according to the popular *maʿannā* choral refrain,[6] they reproduced the metrical scansion of the *fuṣḥā*,

Libnān[i] ḥiṣni ḍ-ḍād[i] ṣāyin[i] ʿizzihā

_ _ ᴗ _ _ _ ᴗ _ ᴗ ᴗ _ ᴗ _

or _ _ ᴗ _ / _ _ ᴗ _ / ᴗ ᴗ _ ᴗ _. Whether the resulting metre is a *rajaz* or a *kāmil* is irrelevant at this point. Without recourse to stress, it is impossible to verify whether we are talking about something resembling the rhythm of *rajaz* or *kāmil.* Only with reference to music and especially musical accent can we have any verification at all. There is no doubt, however, that, quantitatively speaking, the vernacular rendition reproduces the same syllabic content of the *fuṣḥā* scansion. Add to this the fact that

[5] In its ideal form, *al-kāmil* scans according to al-Khalīl: ᴗ ᴗ _ ᴗ _ / ᴗ ᴗ _ ᴗ _ / ᴗ ᴗ _ ᴗ _.

[6] For a musical transcription of the *maʿannā* refrain, see below, pp. 80–81.

one singer differed from the rest by pronouncing *ṣā'in* as *ṣāyin* instead of *ṣāyin*[*i*] (thus causing an amalgamation of the two contiguous short syllables in the third foot, _ _ ᴗ _ instead of ᴗ ᴗ _ ᴗ _), and we get a perfect *rajaz* scansion, at least in terms of quantity. This does not only shed some light on the relationship in *fuṣḥā* between ᴗ ᴗ _ ᴗ _ and _ _ ᴗ _, which al-Khalīl treats as an innocuous licence, but it will also, and for the purpose of this study, clarify the relationship between dialect, music and metre.

Conversely, some *zajals* contain whole lines and stanzas in *fuṣḥā* interspersed with lines in the vernacular. When some of these are read fully as *fuṣḥā*, they destroy the rhythm, but when read as vernacular verses with *fuṣḥā* words interspersed in them, they produce a rhythm reminiscent of the metre which the *fuṣḥā* reading of most of the lines in the *fuṣḥā* idiom recalls. Whole poems of this mixed idiom exist, but they are rare after the first quarter of the twentieth century.[7] They are usually difficult to read because of the non-discriminating *fuṣḥā* orthography and because the reader is called upon to shift constantly from the *fuṣḥā* to the vernacular and vice versa in order to retain the overall metrical and rhythmic pattern. One such example from a poem by Asʿad Jalakh[8] supplies further proof of the derivation of some *zajal* metres from *fuṣḥā* metres:

---

[7] At the beginning of the twentieth century, a series of studies to establish the rules for the Lebanese dialect culminated in the foundation of the 'Emirate of *Zajal*' and the first congress of *zajal* poets in 1945. By 1945, the dialect had been purged of classical words. See Abdel-Nour 1957, 81–91.

[8] The poem is cited by Whaybeh 1952, 180.

Tub w-artajiʿ yā lāhiyan fī jamālihā //
_ _ᴗ_ _ _ᴗ_ _ᴗ_ᴗ_//
'Relent and repent, you who waste time cherishing (this world's) beauty' //

Tafnā wa-ʿan qurbin yakūnu zawāluhā
_ _ ᴗ _ _ _ ᴗ _ᴗ ᴗ_ ᴗ_
'(For) it will die and soon (the world) will end'

which will give _ _ ᴗ _ / _ _ ᴗ _ / _ ᴗ _ ᴗ _ // _ _ ᴗ _ / _ _ ᴗ _ / ᴗ ᴗ _ ᴗ _ or what *fuṣḥā* critics treat as *kāmil* metre. For perfect correspondence with the *kāmil*, however, the first syllable of the third foot of the first hemistich should be made short (i.e. *fī* will have to revert to *fi*). This is precisely where the dialectal reading can affect the change:

Tub w-irtijiʿ yā lāhiyan fi jmālihā
_ _ᴗ_ _ _ᴗ _ _ _ᴗ _

Tifnā wi-ʿan ʾirbin yikūn izwālihā
_ _ ᴗ _ _ _ ᴗ _ _ _ᴗ _

Here we have a perfect *rajaz* scansion without the *kāmil* foot, ᴗ ᴗ _ ᴗ _. Scanning the rest of the poem revealed that the *kāmil* foot appeared only three times. In the following line, the choice of the appropriate idiom is even more important:

Mā dāma fīhā wazīruhā wa-amīruhā //
_ _ᴗ_ _ ᴗ_ᴗ_ ᴗ ᴗ_ᴗ_//
'As long as there is in it cabinet ministers and princes' //

Wa-mulūkuhā wa-junūduhā wa-abṭāluhā
ᴗ ᴗ_ᴗ_ ᴗ ᴗ _ᴗ_ ᴗ _ _ᴗ_
'And kings and soldiers and heroes'

Here the strict *fuṣḥā* reading has jarred the rhythm in the second hemistich beyond recognition. On the other hand, in the vernacular idiom, the second hemistich scans

wi-mlūkihā wi-jnūdiha w-ʾabṭālihā

_ _ᴗ_ _ _ᴗ_ _ _ᴗ_

again yielding a perfect *rajaz* metre.

Likewise, the influence of *al-basīṭ* metre, _ _ ᴗ _ / _ ᴗ _ / _ _ ᴗ _ / _ _, is evident in the earliest recorded *zajal* composed by Sulaymān al-Ashlūḥī around 1298,[9] the date of the destruction of Tripoli (Lebanon) by the Mamlūks. As might be expected, this poem suffers from scribal errors and inaccurate rendition into the graphemes of *fuṣḥā*, but the *basīṭ* metrical pattern is easy to discern in most of its sixty lines, with modifications resulting from the formal morphological characteristics of the Lebanese dialect. If the poem is scanned without a thorough knowledge of this dialect, each line in the poem would yield a different rhythm and a different number of syllables, giving rise to untenable conclusions. For the trained ear, a limited number of readings is possible, and the choice of a particular reading will be determined by the uniform rhythmic pattern that runs throughout the poem. Having determined the basic metrical pattern for some of the more easily read lines, I then selected a reading for every line, which was at once legitimate in the dialect and congruent with the rhythm of the other lines. As it turned out, the number of syllables rarely varied in all the lines and the *basīṭ* feet with their permissible *fuṣḥā* configurations appeared regularly throughout.

---

[9] See Whaybeh 1952, 131–32.

I have chosen four lines[10] to illustrate the scansion method used and the allowable readings in each case.

I. (a) *Yā ḥizn[i] ʾalbī wi-mā yikhlā*[11] *min[i] ḥzānī //*
_ _ ᴗ _ / _ ᴗ _ / _ _ ᴗ _ / _ _ //
'O, sorrow of my heart, and my heart is never without sorrow' //

(b) *Wil-ʾalb[i] mni l-ḥizin shāʿil bi-nīrānī*
_ _ _ / _ ᴗ _ / _ _ ᴗ _ / _ _
'And my heart from sorrow is burning in flames'

or,

(a_2) *Yā ḥizin ʾalbī wi-mā yikhlā min[i] ḥzānī //*
_ ᴗ _ _ / _ ᴗ _ / _ _ ᴗ _ / _ _ //

(b_2) *Wi-l-ʾalib min[i] l-ḥizin shāʿil-ib nīrānī*
_ ᴗ _ ᴗ / _ ᴗ _ / _ ᴗ _ _ / _ _

(a) and (b) are typical *basīṭ* with the first foot of the second hemistich (b) having undergone *qatʿ* ('omission of the short syllable') in _ _ ᴗ _. Hemistich (a_2) has likewise a *basīṭ* pattern, and (b_2) replaces _ _ ᴗ _ with _ ᴗ _ _, a frequent occurrence in a variety of *zajal* metres but completely unacceptable in the *basīṭ* of *fuṣḥā*.

II. (a) *Fī Ṭrābulus kān[i] bid ʾil-ʾawl[i] yā ḥiznī*
_ _ ᴗ _ / _ ᴗ _ / _ _ ᴗ _ / _ _
'It started in Tripoli, O, my sorrow'

---

[10] These correspond to lines 1, 2, 7, and 8 in the poem cited above.

[11] The text reads *ykhallī* ('to allow') rather than *yikhlā* ('to be empty, to be without'). I have opted for the latter reading because it yields better sense, although either reading is suitable for the derivation of a *basīṭ* scansion.

(b) *Wi-l-awl[i] min ʾabl[i] hādha sh-sharḥ[i] qad khānī*
_ _ ᴗ _/ _ ᴗ _/ _ _ ᴗ _/ _ _

'All talk about what happened, before this poem, betrayed the truth'[12]

(a_2) *Fi Ṭrābulus kān[i] bid ʾil-ʾawl[i] yā ḥiznī*
_ _ ᴗ _/ _ ᴗ _/ _ _ ᴗ _/ _ _

(b_2) *Wil awl[i] min ʾabil hādha sh-sharìḥ qad khānī*
_ _ ᴗ _/ ᴗ _ _/ _ ᴗ _ _/ _ _

Here in II. (b_2) the foot ᴗ _ _ replaces _ ᴗ _ because the dialect allows both *ʾabl[i] hādha* (_ ᴗ _ / _) and *ʾabil hādha* (ᴗ _ _ / _), the former a choice being the one usually adopted in the singing or declaiming of the line. Note, however, that lines I. and II. coincide perfectly with the *basīṭ* metre in their first and preferred reading. Also, it is important to note that the ability of the dialect to adapt to various syllabic patterns makes it ideally suited to derive its metres from *fuṣḥā*. In other words, this quality allows the poets of *zajal* a freedom unknown to their counterparts in *fuṣḥā*, who, as al-Khalīl's system indicates, are bound by the more limited reading possibilities of the *fuṣḥā* idiom.

III. (a) *Yā ʿayn[i] khalli l-bukā wi-n-nawḥ[i] ʿādātik*
_ _ ᴗ _/ _ ᴗ _/ _ _ ᴗ _/ _ _

'O, eye, make a habit of weeping and wailing'

(b) *[Iw]-ibkī ʿla n-naṣārā aynimā kān[ī]*
_ _ _/ _ ᴗ _/ _ _ ᴗ _/ _ _

'And cry over the Christians wherever they are'

[12] Here I am not quite sure of the meaning. The word *khāni* does not seem appropriate in the context. If we assume scribal error and change *khāni* to *ḥāni* ('has come about, has become opportune'), the hemistich reads "all talk has become opportune."

IV. (a) *[Iw]-in ibkīti fa damʿ il-ʿayn[i] muḥtariqun*[13]
_ ᴗ _ _ / _ ᴗ _ / _ _ ᴗ _ / ᴗ ᴗ _
'And if you wept, then the tears would be burning'

(b) *[Wi]-in katamti il-bukā fi-l-ʾalb[i] nīrānī*
ᴗ _ ᴗ _ / _ ᴗ _ / _ _ ᴗ _ / _ _
'And if you kept the tears (in the heart), there would be fire in the heart'

Again, here the *basīṭ* metre is evident. In addition to the *qatʿ* in the first foot of III. (b), there is, to use al-Khalīl's terminology, a *khabn* in the last foot of IV. (a) (or _ ᴗ _ become ᴗ ᴗ _), and a simple *ziḥāf* (_ _ ᴗ _ becomes ᴗ _ ᴗ _) in the first foot of IV. (b). It goes without saying that other dialectal readings of these lines are possible, and each reading will give a slightly different quantitative pattern. Only with reference to stress can we ascertain why different syllabic manifestations of feet may or may not play an important role in the determination of rhythm.

Granting then that there are at least three *fuṣḥā* metres, *al-rajaz*, *al-ramal*, and *al-basīṭ*, which the Lebanese *zajal* tradition has utilised, it is important now to identify these and other metres in association with their genres. How many are they altogether? How do they scan? Are they basically quantitative, qualitative, syllabic or a combination of these? What roles do stress and music play in them? What can they tell us about oral vernacular verse in other traditions, Arab and non-Arab? I shall attend to these questions, one by one.

---

[13] *Muḥtariqun* is one of several examples on the missing of idioms. Note the use of desinential inflection, which is never used in dialect.

4. THE ROLE OF STRESS IN THE SCANSION OF *ZAJAL* GENRES

First, a note on stress. Arab and Western critics have in general delegated to stress in Arabic metres an insignificant, or at least a mechanical, role which does not always agree with the morphology of Arabic words appearing separately in the living language or arrayed in metrical patterns.[138] Words in Arabic have a clear stress pattern based on the root system in the language and the morphological shape produced from suffixes, infixes and prefixes. When appearing in a metrical pattern, which itself has its own underlying stresses, they undergo changes resulting from the tension between language stress and metrical stress. This tension is further complicated by the surface pattern of stress produced during the physical performance of speech or recitation.

In his study of stress in Arabic poetry, Kamāl Abū Dīb makes a very plausible case for the underlying stress of Arabic metres which he bases on the succession of units of consonant and vowel combinations, shorter than the feet used by al-Khalīl. Instead of feet, Abū Dīb breaks the units of rhythm into _$_{o}$, a long open or closed syllable represented by Western scansion methods by _, and _ _$_{o}$ (equivalent to a CVC$\bar{V}$ or CVCVC, or ᴗ _), and less frequently _ _ _$_{o}$ or ᴗ ᴗ _. Several things are important to note in Abū Dīb's study. He argues convincingly that stress is more significant than quantity in determining the rhythms of Arabic

[138] See Abū Dīb 1974, 105–25, 327–37.

 https://doi.org/10.11647/OBP.0424.04

poetry, and consequently that lines which do not scan into the feet of al-Khalīl's system or manifest the same quantity of syllables as other lines in a particular poem, can be proven to yield the same rhythm as the other lines with reference to their stress patterns. Moreover, Abū Dīb shows that there is a close correspondence between language stress and metrical stress in that both can be explained in terms of the morphology of Arabic.[139] Length of syllable and syllable position determine at once the rhythm of the word in the language and the rhythm of the metre. This is why the underlying rhythm of metre and the rhythm of language have a high degree of coincidence, unlike say the situation in English language and metre. Through a detailed and, I think, ingenious analysis, Abū Dīb charts out the stress patterns of al-Khalīl's metres demonstrating how the rhythmic vitality of these metres is the net result of the workings of two systems of stress, the poetic and the linguistic. The reader may want to refer to Abū Dīb's analysis of each one of these metres, but for the purpose of this study, only the metres relevant to Lebanese *zajal* will be discussed. These are the *rajaz*, the *basīṭ*, the *sarīʿ*, the *wāfir*, the *ramal* and the *hazaj*.

One warning is in order here: there is, of course, a third important factor which must be considered in this study, and that is the interplay between linguistic and poetic stress on the one hand and that of musical accent, which is ultimately regulated by the laws of music. The patterns of stress in Lebanese *zajal* that

---

[139] Abū Dīb 1974, 289–315.

will eventually emerge will be a further contribution to the rhythmic capacity of Arabic metres.

Leaving aside musical considerations for the present time, I shall list the stress patterns of *rajaz, basīṭ, sarīʿ, wāfir, ramal* and *hazaj*, as Abū Dīb has them. The numbers 1 and 2 designate strong and weak stress, respectively:

(1) *rajaz*

poetic stress $\_\ \underline{1}\ \smile\ \underline{2}\ /\ \_\ \underline{1}\ \smile\ \underline{2}\ /\ \_\ \underline{1}\ \smile\ \underline{2}\ /$

linguistic stress $\underline{1}\ \_\ \smile\ \underline{2}\ /\ \underline{1}\ \_\ \smile\ \underline{2}\ /\ \underline{1}\ \_\ \smile\ \underline{2}\ /$

(2) *basīṭ*

poetic stress $\_\ \underline{1}\ \smile\ \underline{2}\ /\ \underline{1}\ \smile\ \underline{2}\ /\ \_\ \underline{1}\ \smile\ \underline{2}\ /\ \underline{1}\ \smile\ \underline{2}\ /$

linguistic stress $\underline{1}\ \_\ \smile\ \underline{2}\ /\ \underline{1}\ \smile\ \underline{2}\ /\ \underline{1}\ \_\ \smile\ \underline{2}\ /\ \underline{1}\ \smile\ \underline{2}\ /$

(3) *sarīʿ*[140]

poetic stress $\_\ \underline{1}\ \smile\ \underline{2}\ /\ \_\ \underline{1}\ \smile\ \underline{2}\ /\ \underline{1}\ \smile\ \underline{2}\ /$

linguistic stress $\underline{1}\ \_\ \smile\ \underline{2}\ /\ \underline{1}\ \_\ \smile\ \underline{2}\ /\ \underline{1}\ \smile\ \underline{2}\ /$

(4) *ramal*

poetic stress $\underline{1}\ \smile\ \underline{2}\ /\ \_\ \underline{1}\ \smile\ \underline{2}\ /\ \underline{2}\ \underline{2}\ \smile\ \underline{1}\ /\ \underline{2}$

linguistic stress $\underline{2}\ \smile\ \underline{1}\ /\ \underline{1}\ \_\ \smile\ \underline{1}\ /\ \underline{1}\ \_\ \smile\ \underline{2}\ /\ \_$

(5) *wāfir*

poetic stress $\smile\ \_\ \overset{1}{\smile}\ \smile\ \underline{2}\ /\ \smile\ \_\ \overset{1}{\smile}\ \smile\ \underline{2}\ /\ \smile\ \underline{1}\ \underline{2}\ /$

linguistic stress $\smile\ \underline{1}\ \smile\ \smile\ \underline{2}\ /\ \smile\ \underline{1}\ \smile\ \smile\ \underline{2}\ /\ \smile\ \underline{1}\ \underline{2}\ /$

(6) *hazaj*

poetic stress $\smile\ \underline{2}\ \underline{1}\ \_\ /\ \smile\ \underline{2}\ \underline{1}\ \_\ /\ \smile\ \underline{2}\ \underline{1}\ \_\ /$

linguistic stress $\smile\ \underline{1}\ \underline{2}\ \_\ /\ \smile\ \underline{1}\ \underline{2}\ \_\ /\ \smile\ \underline{1}\ \underline{2}\ \_\ /$

This simplified version of stress patterns will be used as a reference point when a *zajal* metre is analysed for its probable derivation from the *fuṣḥā* metre. It will be argued that when a *zajal* metre exhibits the same stress pattern and the same or slightly

---

[140] If $\_\ \_\ \__{o}$ or $\_\ \smile\ \__{o}$ appear in the last foot, they are stressed as follows: $\underline{1}\ \_\ \underline{2}_{o}$, $\underline{2}\ \smile\ \underline{1}_{o}$.

different syllabic configuration as that of a *fuṣḥā* metre, it will be safe to conclude that they are one and the same. How the *zajal* metre is interpreted in song and music is a different matter altogether. For one thing, the particular interpretation will highlight the relative importance of either stress or quantity and will shed further light on the adaptation of *fuṣḥā* metres in *zajal*.

It should be mentioned in passing that Gotthold Weil's study of stress, which he sees implied in al-Khalīl's metrical system, is wrong, in that it is totally incapable of explaining the fluctuation of stress in Arabic poetry as well as in Arabic words which do not contain what he calls 'the rhythmic core' (⏑ _), where he places the stress. So the feet _ _ ⏑ _ (*mustāfʿilun*), _ ⏑ _ (*fāʿilun*), and ⏑ _ _ _ (*mafāʿīlun*) will be according to him stressed as follows: _ _ ⏑ _́, _ ⏑ _́, ⏑ _́ _ _. Metrical exigencies notwithstanding, anyone familiar with Arabic language and poetry will stress the feet differently, placing a secondary stress represented here by ˆ on the rhythmic core: _ _́ ⏑ _̂, _́ ⏑ _̂, ⏑ _̂ _́ _. Dislocation of these stresses does take place in a line of poetry due to the tension between underlying metrical stress and language stress, but never in the way Weil would have us believe.

As has been intimated above, music is essential to *zajal* performances. Many metres are known to poets by their tunes. There are, for example, the tunes of *ʿAl-yādī*, of *Layyā w-layyā*, *ʿArrūzanā*, *Mījanā*, and *ʿAlā dalʿūnā*. The execution of the poetic metre is often determined by the tune it is to be sung to, and the formal characteristics of the metre are in turn modified to fit the tune. Although each *wazn* ('metre') may yield a particular number or assortment of syllables or feet, the tune which is superimposed upon it will allow the poet to vary the number of syllables or the quantity in feet without appearing to undermine the basic metrical structure. Thus, a poem may, when scanned, contain different numbers of syllables in every line, but when sung to a tune, a shortening and lengthening of syllables take place and the words in the poetic line are adjusted to fit the music. The question of what metres are used with what tunes and songs reveals the affinity between others. This, in turn, will make it possible for the critic to account for consistencies or discrepancies in poetic metres when scanned without reference to their accompanying tunes.

There is one important advantage to using musical notations in this work for defining the performance of various metres. Here we are not dealing with scripts of poems, which may be considered in a crude sense as kinds of scores for performing these poems, but which, nevertheless, bring into question the basic issues involved in the relationship of verse to music. Rather, we are dealing with the performances themselves. Professor Lois al-Faruqi, the musicologist who transcribed in musical notation the live performances of most of the *zajal* metres in this study,[141] has elicited her scores from my recordings of the performances of *zajal* poems by well-known Lebanese *zajjāls* and aficionados of *zajal*, producing a descriptive notation in each case. She transcribed the performances in keys that were close, if not identical

[141] The author wishes to acknowledge the late Professor al-Faruqi's contributions to this study. Without her painstaking care in transcribing the musical notations and her rich background in Arabic music, this study would not have been possible.

to sung pitches in order to make them easier to read. Musical accents, notes, pitches and rhythms were all determined by ear, and the transcriptions were rechecked with a slow recording in each case. The transcriptions indicated pitch relationships, the duration of each pitch, and the vocal range of the performers. Some performances were not conducive to a measured representation and, therefore, were transcribed without breaking them into measures of regular and equal length. These are characterised by a particularly ornate or melismatic style (i.e., using several musical notes for a single syllable of verse). Other performances maintained a closer correspondence between numbers of syllables and tones and were based on a musical metre.

Since the performance of a line of poetry involves, among other things, a clear pattern of stress, the descriptive musical notation faithfully reproduces these stresses in the accents of the musical score, thereby providing an excellent opportunity to compare the underlying stress patterns of the poetic metre with the surface pattern of stress produced in performance. Keeping in mind that beat and accent are not the same and do not necessarily coincide, and that syllables in music may at times differ from prosodic syllables due to musical exigencies, the notations still supply important information on the relationship between metre and musical style and between metre and poetic genre.

Careful analysis of the descriptive musical notations prepared for this study shows that the poets of Lebanese *zajal* render their lines in two musical styles, one characterised by a free rhythm, the other by a regularly rhythmed underlay. They divide, in other words, along the two traditional styles of Arabic music:

nathr al-naghamāt and *naẓm al-naghamāt.* The former (literally 'musical prose') refers to 'a vocal or instrumental performance without regularly recurring rhythmic patterns'. The latter, 'ordering of tones', defines 'a musical style based on a traditional melody' and characterised by regular beats.

The *zajal* metres used in the *nathr* style are mostly those of genres which require sophisticated arguments (as in verbal duels) or formal statements about social and political occasions, as well as formal *nasībs* ('amatory preludes'), panegyrics, satirical sketches, boasting, elegiac verse and other sorts of occasional poems. In brief, longer poems with longer metres concerned with various degrees of *iṣābat al-maʿnā* seem to be associated closely with the *nathr* style, and most of their metres bear close resemblance to those of *fuṣḥā* poetry, with frequent licences for which al-Khalīl's system cannot account. Informal, lighter, and shorter poems, such as jokes, some popular songs, counting rhymes (*ʿaddiyyāt*), and verbal tricks, abound in the *naẓm* style, though neither style is differentiated in terms of genre.

The following musical transcriptions of two *maʿannā* and three *qarrādī* pieces illustrate the workings of the two aforementioned styles. They were recorded for this study by Dr Mansour Ajami who himself is a connoisseur of *zajal* and Arabic music. His renditions were compared with live performances of *maʿannā* and *qarrādī* by well-known Lebanese *zajal* poets and were scrutinised for significant melodic differences. For the most part, his recordings proved to be well-executed and quite representative of the *maʿannā* and *qarrādī* sung in Lebanon today.

The first *maʿannā* is composed of four hemistichs with a a, a a rhyme. The first and fourth hemistichs are each repeated once, making a total of six musical lines. The second *maʿannā* (ll. 7–13) is likewise composed of two verses (or four hemistichs) with a similar rhyme scheme. Hemistich one is repeated once and hemistich four is repeated twice. The three *qarrādīs* (ll. 1–4, 5–8, and 9–12) are of four hemistichs each, rhyming a b, a b. In the first one both verses are sung twice. In the second, the first verse is repeated once and the second verse twice. In the third *qarrādī* only the second verse is repeated. The function of repetition at the ends of pieces, though not uniform in Dr Ajami's rendition, is important because it points to the important role that the chorus plays in these two genres. This role is here co-opted by the singer himself due to the absence of choral accompaniment.

Figure 1: *Maʿannā* #1

Recording 1: A recording of this *maʿannā* by the author can be found at https://hdl.handle.net/20.500.12434/352fd301.

Figure 2: *Maʿannā* #2

Recording 2: A recording of this *maʿannā* by the author can be found at https://hdl.handle.net/20.500.12434/0267921a.

Figure 3: *Qarrādī* #1

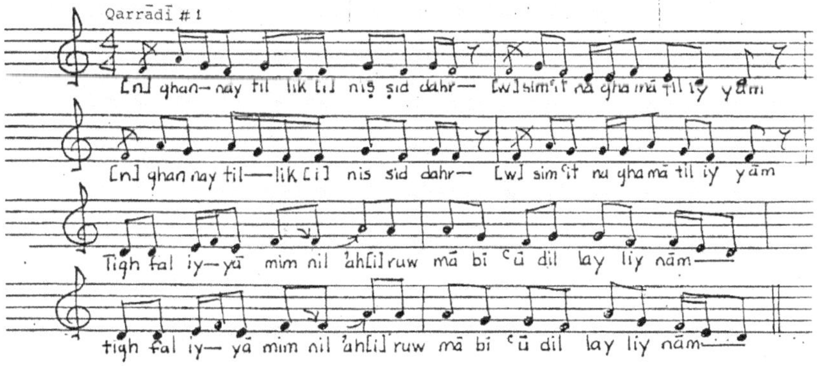

Recording 3: A recording of this *qarrādī* by the author can be found at https://hdl.handle.net/20.500.12434/cf56cbf1.

Figure 4: *Qarrādī #2*

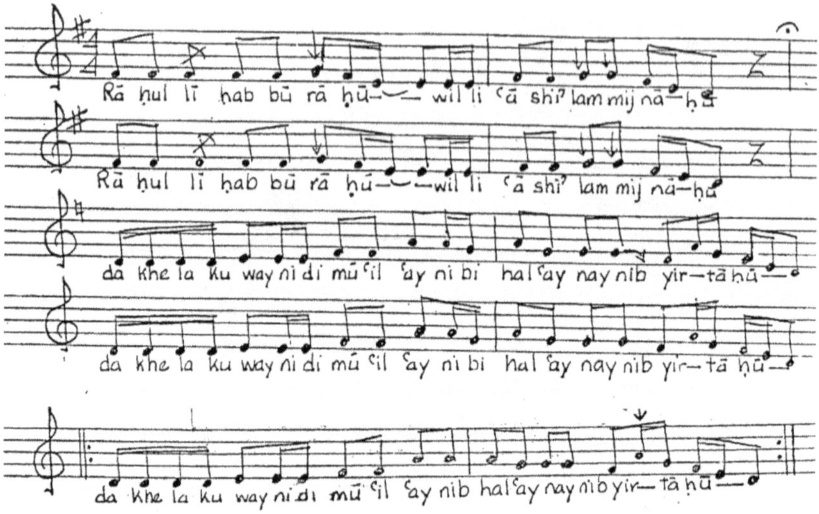

Recording 4: A recording of this *qarrādī* by the author can be found at https://hdl.handle.net/20.500.12434/d2c44fef.

Figure 5: *Qarrādī #3*

Recording 5: A recording of this *qarrādī* by the author can be found at https://hdl.handle.net/20.500.12434/359dcb61.

In the transcriptions of *maʿannā* there is a greater diversity of note durations than in *qarrādī*. There are grace notes, trilled notes, dotted notes, 16th notes, 8th notes, quarter notes, variants of these in triplets, plus mordents and other ornaments. In the *qarrādī* examples, on the other hand, all we have are grace notes,

16th notes, and 8th notes, resulting in a much simpler rhythmic structure with more reserved melodic embellishment. For the most part, a single syllable in *qarrādī* corresponds to a single tone. Long syllables correspond to 8th notes, while short syllables correspond to 16th notes, which are half the value of 8th notes. Thus two musical shorts are equivalent to a long, as is roughly the case in poetry. Moreover, *maʿannā* exhibits an irregular number of beats and notes in a phrase, while each *qarrādī* phrase generally has the same number of beats. A *waqfa* (pause of silence) makes the phrase endings precise in *maʿannā*, while in *qarrādī* half or full cadences end the various phrases corresponding to hemistichs. *Maʿannā* abounds in triplet figures, but duple combinations dominate in *qarrādī*.

Melodic movement also differs in the two styles. In *maʿannā*, descending movements characterise the melodic line, except for occasional rises at the beginning of phrases. Conversely, *qarrādī* reveals many arched melodic contours in its phrases with descending melodic movement prominent at the end of lines. In both genres there is a tendency to return at the end of each phrase to a tone of stability (*qarār*). The uniformity of syllables in *qarrādī* (being mostly long) affords the performer the freedom to impose a strongly evident musical metre, without distorting the meaning of the verse. In *maʿannā*, on the other hand, the variation in syllabic quantity and the use of multi-tones for a single long syllable generates a freedom of musical duration, while preserving the clarity of the verbal meanings. There is strong evidence for the importance of syllable quantity in the *maʿannā* genre, as well as a close correspondence between long syllables and long musical durations on the one hand, and between short syllables and short musical durations, on the other. In the event of durational discrepancies, other elements play a compensatory role. Some of these are: (1) position within a group (earlier positions within a musical measure are generally stronger), (2) pitch (higher tones are usually stronger than lower, as is evident in line 5, first *maʿannā*), (3) ornamentation (provides accentuation), (4) change of prevailing melodic direction (melodic direction will be more outstanding), and (5) a leap to a tone makes that tone more prominent. In sum, poetic metre in *maʿannā* takes precedence over musical metre while the reverse is true in *qarrādī*.

As might be expected, stress in *maʿannā* (and all genres rendered in the *nathr* style) is irregular, since the poet freely manipulates it to accord with semantic considerations. Of course it may, at times, coincide with underlying metrical stress, but it is neither mechanical nor characterised by regularity. Its orientation is towards the message, because the content (i.e., poetry) is more important than the formal structure (i.e., music). Conversely, the metres rendered in *naẓm*, such as *qarrādī*, have a strict rhythmic pattern imposed by a musical metre. While singing *qarrādī*, the poet is in effect producing a neutral realization of the following trochaic pattern: _́ _ _́ _ _́ _ _́. The appearance of short syllables, as we shall see momentarily, is not infrequent in *qarrādī*, and they always count in the measure.

When they fall in the position of an accented syllable, they are themselves stressed to preserve the metre. By and large, this strict observance of a superimposed stress pattern external to the poetry does not seem to affect the meaning or slur the morphemes. The infrequency of extra-long syllables (except at the end of hemistichs) guards against such likelihood.

A general survey[142] of close to two hundred examples of *maʿannā* recorded for this study revealed that the poets consistently render their lines in an improvised manner in stanzas ranging from two to twenty lines. The end of each improvisation is signalled by a regularity that was missing in the preceding lines. This is picked up and emphasised by the chorus in a rhythmic (metric) style based on a traditional folk tune, repeated twice. If the particular poem is part of a verbal duel, the opponent enters with his own improvisation and cues in the chorus in similar manner. In all cases, the chorus sings the same folk tune throughout the verbal duel, sometimes with slight melodic variations, but always according to the musical metre. Although each of the poet's lines is based on the same poetic metre, the musical rendition of the lines becomes increasingly complicated as he proceeds to the choral entry. Unlike the chorus, however, which renders only one rhythmic version of the metre, the poet makes full use of the licences sanctioned by the dialect, rarely following the stress pattern established by the chorus. When the poet starts singing, he does so without choral introduction, often repeating the first hemistich or line to gain a sense of the musical rhythm

[142] The survey includes *maʿannā* poems recorded from live performances, in addition to several *maʿannā* pieces recorded during interviews with living *zajal* poets. Here again I wish to thank the late Professor Israel Katz for his help in transcribing the choral renditions of many of the aforementioned *maʿannā* poems.

which he knows well. Instead of a verbal choral participation, a rhythmic pattern is established by a combination of accompanying clapping, and/or drum and tambourine beats supplied by the chorus. In other words, the *maʿannā* poem is, as it were, framed by a regular metrical rhythm which guides the poet in his free improvisation of the message he wishes to convey.

The recorded solo-choral renditions revealed that the metrical pattern and the refrain time established by the chorus were the same in all samples. With the help of the well-known musicologist Professor Israel Katz, it was possible to derive a proto-tune for all the performances:[143]

Figure 6: Proto-tune

This proto-tune was compared with the rendition of musical line 6 of the first *maʿannā* piece above, which was improvised by Dr Ajami as a substitute for a choral response. When he was asked to play the role of the chorus, he did so by starting on the downbeat instead of the upbeat where the chorus would always start. Thus he misplaced the accents on the phrases as they have been sung by the chorus, misconstruing at the same time the rhythm of the opening syllables by giving them a mensuration twice as

[143] The proto-tune was derived through careful screening of solo-choral renditions by varying the speeds of those renditions in order to arrive at a description of their common features. Note that bar lines in the musical transcription point at once to a musical accent and poetic stress on following syllables.

fast as that of the original tune. This was because, unlike the typical choral rendition which followed the poet after he had come to a complete stop, he did not pause and instead continued the rhythmic flow of his last line of improvisation. The same change of alignment occurred when the musicologist asked the author of this study to perform the role of the chorus.

Figure 7: Line 6 of *maʿannā* #1

Ajami and author's version: Proto-tune:

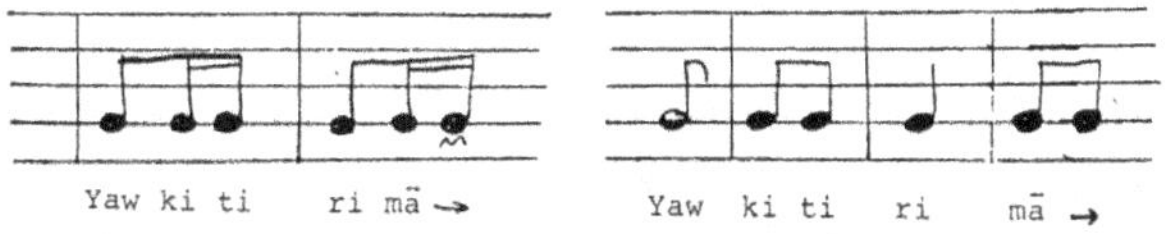
Yaw ki ti ri mā
Yaw ki ti ri mā

For the sake of comparison, the methodology involved two separate scansions. The first was derived from the musical notation of the performance; the second from a poetic scansion of the transcribed text, overlooking, as a rule, the role of stress. What is important here is that we are working from a recorded performance, taking cognizance of the poet's and the chorus' renditions from a musical point of view. After transcribing the performance, we analysed the musical notation, from which we derived a poetic scansion. Upon the musical scansion we superimposed a poetic one according to the established *fuṣḥā* scansion rules. This enabled us to note the coincidence between musical accent and poetic stress. Since we were dealing throughout with a live performance, the music captured for us how the poetic lines were rendered. Matching the musical and poetic scansions, we obtained one of the two typical stress patterns of the *fuṣḥā rajaz* metre as described quantitatively by al-Khalīl. Line 6 gives the following breakdown of syllables:

yaw ki ti / ri mā / byin ʾā / li la ʾ / ʾā wim / ba lā
_ ⏑ ⏑ / _ ⏑ ⏑ / _ ⏑ ⏑ / ⏑ ⏑ ⏑ ⏑ / ⏑ ⏑ ⏑ ⏑ / ⏑ ⏑ _

The line has the following metrical scansion:

yaw ki ti   ri mā   byin ʾā   li laʾ   ʾā wim   ba lā
_ ⏑⏑[144]   ⏑ _   _ _   ⏑ _   _ _   ⏑ _

or, in terms of feet: _ ⏑⏑ ⏑ _ / _ _ ⏑ _ / _ _ ⏑ _. Superimposed upon each other,

	yaw ki ti	*ri mā*	*byin ʾā*	*li laʾ*	*ʾā wim*	*ba lā*
music	_ ⏑ ⏑ /	_ ⏑ ⏑ /	_ ⏑ ⏑ /	⏑ ⏑ ⏑ ⏑ /	⏑ ⏑ ⏑ ⏑ /	⏑ ⏑ _
poetry	_ ⏑⏑ /	⏑ _ /	_ _ /	⏑ _ /	_ _ /	⏑ _

The accent at the beginning of each musical unit or measure coincides with the first long and the short syllable of each poetic foot. Thus the metrical rendering reveals the following stress pattern: _́ _ ⏑́ _ / _́ _ ⏑́ _ / _́ _ ⏑́ _.

This pattern of stress is, however, unusual and quite different from the rhythm of the *rajaz* metre.[145]

If the same hemistich is superimposed upon the proto-tune in the following manner,

	yaw	*ki ti ri*	*mā byin*	*ʾā li*	*laʾ ʾā*	*wim ba*	*lā*
Proto-tune	_ /	⏑ ⏑ _ /	⏑ ⏑ _ /	⏑ ⏑ /	⏑ ⏑ ⏑ ⏑ /	⏑ ⏑ ⏑ ⏑ /	_
Poetic metre	_ /	⏑⏑ _ /	_ _ /	_ ⏑ /	_ _ /	_ ⏑	_

the results obtained are

_ _́ ⏑ _́ / _ _́ ⏑ _́ / _ _́ ⏑ _́ instead of
_́ _ ⏑́ _ / _́ _ ⏑́ _ / _́ _ ⏑́ _

---

[144] *Kit ri* and *ki ti ri* (_ ⏑ and ⏑ ⏑ ⏑) are possible in the vernacular reading where a long syllable is often equivalent to two short ones: _ = ⏑ ⏑. The symbol ⏑⏑ (underlined) is being used to represent this case.

[145] The stress pattern of *rajaz* is _ _́ ⏑ _́ / _ _́ ⏑ _́ / _ _́ ⏑ _́. See Abū Dīb 1974, 327–43.

The former stress pattern is the one commonly associated with *rajaz* and may result from Dr Ajami's and the author's unconscious adherence to that poetic tradition.

It is to be noted that the first hemistich (repeated) of the *maʿannā* described above is the closest of all the hemistichs to the musical accents of the proto-tune or choral rendition. It differs from them only in the last poetic foot, where musical accent coincides with poetic stress on the first and fourth syllables, rather than on the second and the fourth, and where the second foot loses the expected stress on the fourth syllable:

Line 1	*Tis la mī lī ki tir mā fī kī ḥa lā*
music	_ ᴗ / _ _ / ᴗ ᴗ _ / _ _ ᴗ / _
poetry	_ / _ ᴗ / _ _ / _ ᴗ _ / _ _ ᴗ / _
	ᴗ _ _
poetic metre's stress pattern	_ _́ ᴗ _́ / _ _́ ᴗ _ / _́ _ ᴗ _́

Taking into consideration that the *rajaz* foot often exhibits the stress pattern _́ _ ᴗ _́, the close resemblance of this line to the choral version suggests that the poet starts a *maʿannā* piece with clear consciousness of the metre on which he is to improvise in the hemistichs and lines that follow. It is the rhythmic-metric introduction (clapping and tambourine beats) that cues in the poet at the beginning of his improvisation. In addition to this, poets of *zajal* start by humming the proto-tune as the clapping and tambourine beats introduce the *maʿannā*.

* * *

There is a great discrepancy between the way a line of *maʿannā* is read or declaimed freely by the poet and the way in which it is sung by the chorus with reference to a well-known tune. Reading involves, first, a knowledge of the dialect and, second, a sense of metrical correctness if it is to succeed at all. Proper reading is therefore synonymous with the poet's free, improvisatory method and, like the poet's rendition, it is interested first and foremost in conveying clearly the content or meaning of the line or lines. Without constant reference, however, to the chorus' proto-tune, the procrustean myth is revived and the reader may distort the metre and miscount the syllables. Take, for example, the following lines:

(a) *Shū ʾāl Bin Ḥamdān yā ʾarḍ ismaʿī*
— —́o —   — —́o — —́ —ᴗ́ —
'What did Ibn Ḥamdān say? Listen, ye world!'

(a^{i}) *ʾĀl ʿam bihaddidni w-bizindū yiddiʿī*
—́o — ᴗ — —́ —   ᴗ —́ — — ᴗ́ —
'He thinks he is threatening me and bragging about his arms (strength)'

(b) *Mish ʿārif il mā ʾilt li-sh-shams iṭlaʿī*
— —́ᴗ — — —́o — —́   — ᴗ —́
'Does he not know if I don't say to the sun, "Rise!"'

(b^{i}) *Biṭṭīʿ w-ibtirkaʿ idhā ʾilt irkaʿī*
— —́o   — —́ —   ᴗ́ — —́ — ᴗ —́
'It will obey and will kneel down if I say, "Kneel!"'

(c) *[W]-mish ʿārif il-manbar ṭiliʿ min maʾlaʿī*
— —́ᴗ — —́ — ᴗ́ — —   —́ ᴗ —
'And does he not know that the pulpit arose from my quarry?'

(c^{i}) *[W]-awṣ il-adaḥ khātimi zghīr ib-iṣbaʿī*
—́ — ᴗ́ —   —́ ᴗ — —́   — —́ ᴗ —
'And that the rainbow is a little ring around my finger?'

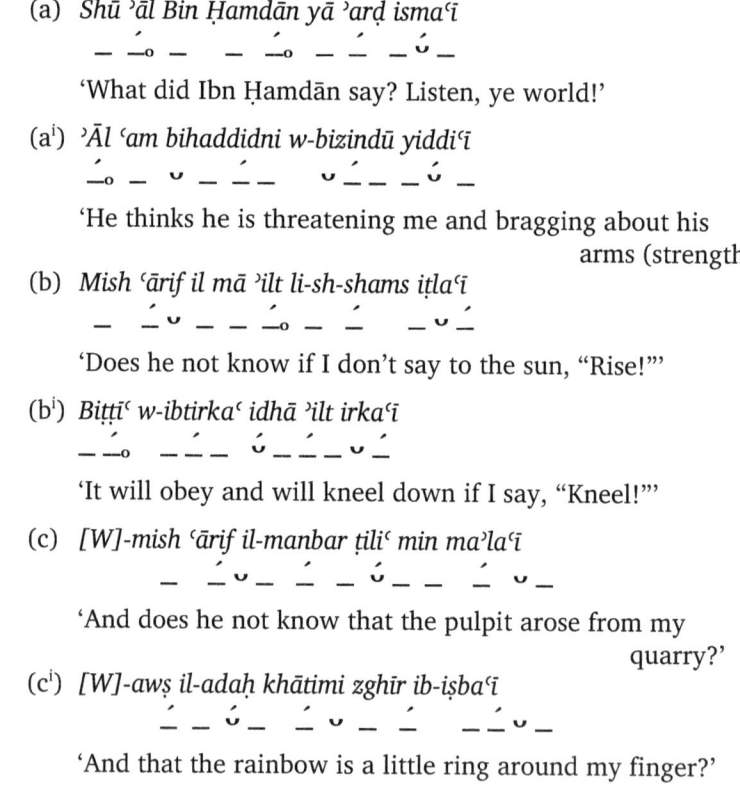

These lines are from a famous verbal duel whose scansion represents the way the poet delivered them. Hemistich (a) is composed of ten syllables, (b) and (b^{i}) of eleven each, and the rest of twelve each. Only hemistichs (a), (b), and (b^{i}) have, as rendered by the poet, extra-long syllables. It is hard to detect in (a), (b), and (b^{i}) a clear pattern of feet, but the foot _ _ ⏑ _, repeated three times, seems to appear in the rest of the hemistichs. It is possible to divide (a) into _ _ _ / _ _ _ / _ _ ⏑ _, (b) into _ _ ⏑ _ / _ _ _ / _ _ ⏑ _, and (b^{i}) into _ _ _ / _ _ ⏑ _ / _ _ ⏑ _, and consider the appearance of _ _ _ as an acceptable rhythmic alternative to _ _ ⏑ _. Such a possibility, though not sanctioned by traditional metrics, assumes a high probability with reference to the choral version. Sung as a refrain by the chorus, hemistichs (a), (b), and (b^{i}) exhibit the following syllabic and stress features:

(a) *Shū ʾāl[i] Bin Ḥamdān[i] yā ʾarḍ ismaʿī*
_ _́ ⏑ _́ / _ _́ ⏑ _́ / _ _́ ⏑ _́

(b) *Mish ʿārif il mā ʾilt[i] li-sh-shams iṭlaʿī*
_ _́ ⏑ _́ / _ _́ ⏑ _́ / _ _́ ⏑ _́

(b^{i}) *Biṭṭīʿ[i] w-ibtirkaʿ idhā ʾilt irkaʿī*
_ _́ ⏑ _́ / _ _́ ⏑ _́ / _ _́ ⏑ _́

This, as we have seen above, is the most common stress pattern of the *rajaz* metre. On the other hand, the number of stresses in the poet's version ranges between four and five per hemistich and their position varies from one hemistich to another. To put it differently, the poet interprets the rhythm of *rajaz* liberally, often going against the underlying metrical stress.

The chorus often breaks extra-long syllables into longs and shorts (_ ⏑). This is at least true of the lines above. At times, however, even the poet may render an extra-long syllable not into a long and a short, but into a short and a long (⏑ _),

ʿĀwad sa ʾāni d-dahir kāsāt il-ḥimām
— — ᴗ —/ — ᴗ — —/ — — ᴗ —o
'Time has once again given me to drink cups of death'

opting for the permissible dialectal reading of *dahr* as *da* and *hir* instead of *dah* and *ri* as the chorus would sing it:

ʿĀwad sa ʾāni dahr[i] kāsāt il-ḥimām
— — ᴗ —/— — ᴗ —/— — ᴗ —o

The second foot in the poet's version is — ᴗ — —, not — — ᴗ —, which is an unacceptable replacement for a *rajaz* in *fuṣḥā*.

Now consider the poet's rendition of the second hemistich of this line:

W-il-basiṭ ṣār mamnūʿ ʿannī w-iḥtajāb
— ᴗ — —/ — —o —/ — — ᴗ —o
'And happiness become forbidden to me and has disappeared'

Three things should be noticed here. First, the foot — ᴗ — — appears at the beginning. Second, the word *ṣār* ('became, has become') and the syllable *nūʿ* in *mamnūʿ* are both extra-long. Third, the long syllable *jab* in *iḥtajab* ('to be veiled, to be eclipsed, to disappear') is lengthened to *jāb* in order to anticipate the end-rhyme words in the rest of the poem. Despite this lengthening of the last syllable for poetic necessity, this hemistich resembles the previous one in that it exhibits the same modifications of the *rajaz* foot. Interestingly enough, the chorus sings the lines according to the poetic metre even at the expense of changing the quantity of syllables:

W-il-basṭ[i] ṣār mamnūʿ[i] ʿannī w-iḥtajāb[146]
— — ᴗ — — — ᴗ — — — ᴗ —

[146] Note that the chorus often renders the last long syllable extra-long.

shortening *ṣār* from an extra-long syllable to a long one. Yet appearing in a different position in a line, the word *ṣār* is sung by the chorus as *ṣā* and *ri*, as was the case with the extra-long syllables cited above. My research has shown that such an occurrence is not so much the result of *ṣār* (or for this matter any extra-long syllable) being preceded by another extra-long syllable, *basṭ* ('happiness'), as much as it is due to the regular rhythm of the tune to which it is sung. This confirms the importance of knowing this tune in determining whether an extra-long syllable divides into _ ᴗ, or ᴗ _, or _. In the same way, the poet's rendition of *maʿannā*, albeit free and *nathr*ish in style, cannot be scanned poetically without knowledge of the music which the poet 'composes', as it were, as he sings his lines.

In the above examples, the chorus produces an ideal *rajaz fuṣḥā* metre, with clear quantitative feet and a regular stress pattern in every foot. Sometimes, however, the quantity changes while the stress pattern remains constant. Depending on the syllables' characteristics, the chorus may itself substitute a variety of feet for the standard *rajaz* foot, although these would be unacceptable substitutions in al-Khalīl's system. The following lines, sung to the choral proto-tune, cover, I believe, most,[147] if not all, of the possible foot variations in *maʿannā*:

(a) *Yā wilād il-fann[i] kūnu m-ʾaddabbīn*
_́ ᴗ _́ / _ _́ ᴗ _́ / _ _́ ᴗ _́o
'O, little children of the art (*zajal*), be polite!'

---

[147] One variation, ᴗ ᴗ _ ᴗ _, is also quite frequent in some dialectal readings.

(a^{i}) *[W]-lā ti'ūlū ṣāri fī sinn il-kabār*[148]

_́ ⏑ _́ / _ _́ ⏑ _́ / _ _́ ⏑ _́o

'And don't say he has become advanced in years'

(b) *Ba'di minn il-'arḍi bitzīd il-'anīn*

_́ ⏑ _́ / _ _́ ⏑ _́ / _ _́ ⏑ _́o

'After me (my death), the earth will increase its moans'

(b^{i}) *Wi-ni ḍrabt iṣ-ṣakhr ibdarrīhī ghubār*[149]

⏑ _́ _ _ / _ _́ _ / _́ _ ⏑ _́o

'And if I hit rocks, I grind them to dust'

(c) *Ma zāli-hashmālī b-itiz 'if 'al-yamīn*

⏑ _́ ⏑ _́ / _ _́ ⏑ _́ / _ _́ ⏑ _́o

'As long as my left hand can clap on my right one'

(c^{i}) *Mā bidārī lā kibīr iw-lā zighīr*

_́ ⏑ _́ / _ _́ ⏑ _́ / _ _́ ⏑ _́o

'I will not pay attention to anyone, big or small'

Normally the chorus begins with a vocable or meaningless syllable, such as *yaw* or *iw*, but occasionally it starts with the first syllable of the poet's line, shortening the expected foot _ _ ⏑ _ to _ ⏑ _ without jarring the rhythm. The traditional scansion of the *fuṣḥā* system cannot account for such quantitative changes, although al-Khalīl did note, without explaining fully, such occurrence in *fuṣḥā* poetry.[150] In the stanza cited above, hemistichs (a), (a^{i}), (b), and (c) substitute _́ ⏑ _́ for _ _́ ⏑ _́ in the first foot, and

---

148 *Kabar* here at the end of the hemistich is rendered as *kabār* to reflect the choral rendition, at the expense of the morphological and semantic meaning of the word.

149 Variant: *win ḍarabtiṣ* _ ⏑ _ _.

150 Since al-Khalīl's system is based on the poetry he heard recited or sung, such quantitative changes at the beginning of the lines of particular metres must have been frequent.

(b^{i}) contains — ⏑́ — —́ (in the variant reading of the first foot), —́ — —́, and ⏑ —́ — —́, which, with the exception of — — — (and then in only one place in the *rajaz* line), cannot be considered *ziḥāfs* or *iʿlāls* of the recurrent *rajaz* foot. The stress patterns, however, seem to coincide in all feet:

—	—́	⏑	—́
⏑	—́	—	—́
—	⏑́	—	—́
	—́	—	—́
	—́	⏑	—́

It would be useless to seek an answer to these substitutions by appealing to quantitative considerations, or to speak of feet in al-Khalīl's sense of the word. Only with reference to coincidence of stress can we understand these alternative rhythmic units and can we in fact explain away numerous *ziḥāfs* and *iʿlāls* attributed to Arabic *fuṣḥā* metres, as Kamāl Abū Dīb shows in his study. This is not to say that quantity is not an important characteristic of *maʿannā*, other *zajal* metres and *fuṣḥā* metrics, but it is important to realise that stress is the main determinant of rhythm.

Of course, the poet's free improvisatory rendition of these lines would have a less predictable stress pattern since, as we have seen, his purpose is *iṣābat al-maʿnā*. Nevertheless, an account of the poet's version will elucidate matters further. In what follows, I shall indicate the place of pauses by placing the letter p after each pause. As we shall see, two new feet, — — and ⏑ — —, will appear in the poet's rendition:

(a) *Yā wlād il-fann kūnu m-ʾaddabīn*

— — — — —— —⏑ —o

(a^{i}) *[W]-lā t'ūlū ṣār fī sinn il-kabār*

— ———o — — — ᴗ —o

(b) *Baʿid minn il-ʾariḍ bitzīd il-ʿanīn*

ᴗ — — — ᴗ — ——— — ᴗ —o

(b^{i}) *Wi-niḍrabt iṣ-ṣakhir bdarrīhi ghubār*

ᴗ — — —ᴗ — — —ᴗ ᴗ —o

(c) *Mā zālha shmālī btiz ʾif ʿal-yamīn*

— —o — —— — —— ᴗ —o

(c^{i}) *Mā bdārī lā kbīr iw-lā zghīr*

— ——— — — — —o

or,

(a) —́ p —́ / — —́ p —́ / — —́ ᴗ —́
(a^{i}) —́ p —́ / — —́ p —́ / — — ᴗ —́
(b) ᴗ́ — p —́ / — ᴗ́ — — / — — ᴗ —́
(b^{i}) ᴗ — —́ p / — ᴗ́ — — / —́ ᴗ ᴗ —́
(c) — —́ — p / —́ — — / — —́ ᴗ —́
(c^{i}) —́ p —́ / — —́ p —́ / — —́ p —́[151]

Here, on the other hand, we have an indication that quantity is quite important. If we substitute a short or a long syllable to every pause, we get a scansion not unlike that obtained from the chorus' version. It is as though the poet is less free in his interpretation of the lines' quantity than in his observance of semantic stress.

It goes without saying that syllable number is not fixed in the lines, not even in the more regulated choral version. There is simply no alternative to hearing *maʿannā* declaimed freely by the poet and sung more regularly by the chorus. Using the printed text and syllable count as sources for metrical description is

[151] The stress pattern in the preceding lines has been obtained after several readings by three aficionados of *zajal.*

fraught with dangers, even if allowances are made for the *nathr* or prosaic quality of *maʿannā*. One more caution is necessary. Some critics of Lebanese *zajal*[152] assume without proof or justification that *maʿannā* may appear in the *wāfir fuṣḥā* metre supposedly in the form ᴗ _ _ _ / ᴗ _ _ _ / ᴗ _ _[153] or in the *basīṭ*, the more popular form of which is _ _ ᴗ _ / _ ᴗ _ / _ _ ᴗ _ / _ _. There is here, it seems to me, a confusion between *maʿannā* as a general term for a love poem and *maʿannā* as a particular metre well-known to *zajal* poets. The appearance of the foot ᴗ _ _ _, as the examples above have shown, may have something to do with that, but this is a pervasive problem which the strict application of quantitative scansion techniques cannot hope to address. Indeed some *maʿannā* lines may have one or more _ ᴗ _ _, the basic foot of *ramal* metre, but this does not qualify them to be *ramal* because the stress pattern may be quite alien to that of the *ramal*.[154] The temptation to force _ ᴗ _ / _ _ ᴗ _ / _ _ ᴗ _ into _ ᴗ _ _ / _ ᴗ _ _ / _ ᴗ _, and end up with a *ramal* in which the last foot suffers *ḥadhf* ('deletion of the last long syllable'), is all too real since no *rajaz* line in the traditional system may start with _ ᴗ _ instead of _ _ ᴗ _.

Still, some claim that *maʿannā* scans in the *kāmil* metre (ᴗ _ ᴗ _ / ᴗ ᴗ _ ᴗ _ / ᴗ ᴗ _ ᴗ _). The *kāmil* presents an interesting problem. Among others, al-Khalīl admits that this metre may

[152] See, for example, Abdel-Nour 1957, 108.

[153] Curiously enough, the meter *hazaj* may indeed exhibit the following order of feet: ᴗ _ _ _ / ᴗ _ _ _ / ᴗ _ _ _.

[154] For the poetic and linguistic stress of the *ramal* meter see Abū Dīb 1974, 339.

undergo a *ziḥāf*, changing every ⏑ ⏑ _ ⏑ _ into _ _ ⏑ _. In other words, we can consider _ _ ⏑ _ / _ _ ⏑ _ / _ _ ⏑ _, which is clearly a *rajaz* line, a *kāmil* line if the line is found in a poem in *kāmil* where only one foot in the whole poem is a *kāmil* foot (⏑ ⏑ _ ⏑ _). This is one of the main problems with al-Khalīl's system and one which will always plague metricians who subscribe to the purely quantitative analysis of Arabic poetry. Stress seems to me to be a better measure of the rhythms of Arabic poetry in general.

Abdel-Nour appears to be aware of this problem, although, he, like many writers on *zajal*, does not see in stress a possible answer to such untenable assumptions by al-Khalīl:[155]

> Dans une enquête que nous avons menée auprès des poètes, la plupart des réponses écrites que nous avons reçues confirmaient l'idée que le *maʿannā* est composé sur le mètre *kāmil* dont le paradigme en poésie classique est le suivant: ⏑ ⏑ _ ⏑ _ / ⏑ ⏑ _ ⏑ _ / ⏑ ⏑ _ ⏑ _, deux fois, et qui subit généralement un altération consistant dans le changement de: ⏑ ⏑ _ ⏑ _ en: _ _ ⏑ _. Par ailleurs, ce mètre ainsi modifié s'assimile au *rajaz*.... Or, dans tous les poèmes que nous avons examinés, il nous a été impossible de trouver cette dernière forme.
>
> (In a survey we conducted among poets, most of the written responses we received confirmed the idea that the *maʿannā* is composed in the *kāmil* metre, whose paradigm in classical poetry is as follows: ⏑ ⏑ _ ⏑ _ / ⏑ ⏑ _ ⏑ _ / ⏑ ⏑ _ ⏑ _, twice, and which generally undergoes an alteration consisting of changing: ⏑ ⏑ _ ⏑ _ to: _ _ ⏑ _. Furthermore, this modified metre assimilates to the *rajaz*.... However, in

[155] Abdel-Nour 1957, 97.

all the poems we examined, it was impossible for us to find this latter form.)

It is unfortunate that Abdel-Nour bases his judgment in the last sentence on written examples of *maʿannā* compositions. That feet of *kāmil* are quite frequent in sung *maʿannā*, explains in large part the insistence of some poets that *maʿannā* is indeed related to the *kāmil* as it is imperfectly explained by al-Khalīl and as it is, as a result, confused with *rajaz* by educated *zajal* poets and traditional critics of Arabic metres. Take, for example, the following *maʿannā* hemistich[156] which is read as follows:

> *[B]yitzakkar it-tārīkh[i] ʿarkit bat*[157] *Mirī*
> — — ⏑ —/ — — ⏑ —/ — — ⏑ —
> 'History will remember the battle of Beit Mirī'

yielding a strict succession of *rajaz* feet. But, sung to the choral proto-tune, its last foot changes into

> *[B]yitẓakkar it-tārīkh[i] ʿarkit[i] bat Mirī*
> — — ⏑ —/ — — ⏑ —/ ⏑ ⏑ — ⏑ —

Taking into consideration al-Khalīl's assumption that one foot of *kāmil* qualifies a line to be in the *kāmil* metre, we could perhaps understand the alleged relationship of *maʿannā* to this metre. As we have seen above, however, quantity alone fails to explain such anomalies. On the other hand, if the stress pattern in a *kāmil* foot coincides precisely with that of the *rajaz* foot, the two feet will

---

[156] The hemistich is from the famous verbal duel between the groups of Zaghlūl al-Dāmūr and Mūsa Zghayb at Deir al-Qalʿa in the village of Beit Mirī, Lebanon, in 1971. More than 10,000 people attended the duel.

[157] The term *bat* is a dialectal contraction of *bayt* ('house').

be shown to be interchangeable, quantity notwithstanding. Thus, in this case, in particular, ⏑ ⏑ – ⏑ – receives stress on the third and fifth syllables ⏑ ⏑ –́ ⏑ –́, which appears to be rhythmically similar to – –́ ⏑ –́. Besides being a more convincing way of explaining the rhythmic components of *rajaz* and *kāmil*, such reference to quality rather than quantity eliminates the so-called *ziḥāfs* and *iʿlāls* that complicate al-Khalīl's system.[158] This is not to detract critics from al-Khalīl's monumental achievement. It is rather a comment on any system's ability to deal with exceptions to its general, and often restrictive rules. It is, above all, a proof that al-Khalīl did indeed base his system on heard or sung verse, despite the fact that his system could not accommodate every deviation from the rules.

There remains the question of the form or forms of the *maʿannā* poem. When the word *maʿannā* is not used to mean Lebanese *zajal* in general, it is specifically cited as a composition of a number of verses ranging from two to twenty or more in a metre called invariably by *zajjāls*, *qawwāls*, and poets of *zajal* the *maʿannā* metre.[159] This metre, as we have seen, shares with the *rajaz* of *fuṣḥā* poetry most of its formal characteristics, differing from it only in the licences that the morphology and phonology of the vernacular permit. Reference is usually made to a *bayt* of *maʿannā* (two verses of two hemistichs each) or a *raddet maʿannā* ('a response in *maʿannā*'). The first verse is called a *sharḥa* (lit. 'long, thin slice'), while the second, which contains the bulk of

---

[158] See Abū Dīb 1974, 327–45.

[159] The poets recognise the metre as *baḥr al-maʿannā*.

the response, is called a *raddeh*. Both terms, *bayt maʿannā* and *raddet maʿannā*, were used interchangeably until the 1940s, mostly in the popular verbal duels between the various *zajjāls*. The typical *bayt* had the rhyme scheme a a b a. From the 1940s on, a new development took place.[160] The *bayt* gave way to the *maʿannā* stanza which ranged between six and twenty verses rhyming a a, a a, a a, etc., b a. In verbal duels, this form is used to signal the next dueller that his turn to recite has come. The signal is, in effect, this sudden change from rhyme a to b, a closure of a sort clearly understood by both poets and audience.

This is the form of *maʿannā* in the restricted sense of the term. There is what is called *qaṣīd maʿannā* which many critics treat as *maʿannā* proper,[161] though the word *qaṣīd* seems to be a clear indication of a genre distinction. The *qaṣīd maʿannā*, as I have been able to determine, is a *qaṣīd* which uses the *maʿannā* metre, but differs from *maʿannā* as genre in the many rhyme schemes in which it is executed. Therefore, these rhyme schemes will be discussed below in the section devoted to *qaṣīd*.

---

[160] Credit for the new development should go to Zaghlūl al-Dāmūr and his *jawqa*, who introduced the *maʿannā* stanza to Lebanese *zajal*.

[161] See, for example, Whaybeh 1952, 64–65.

5. *QARRĀDĪ* AND ITS VARIOUS MANIFESTATIONS

It is often assumed that *qarrādī* had its beginnings in the translated hymns of Saint Ephrem the Syrian (d. 373) who is credited with a mass of metrical homilies and hymns on numerous theological subjects.[1] These hymns, called *Afrāmiyyāt* after their composer, are distinguished by a particular tune which seems to have preserved the original Syriac prototype. The *laḥn afrāmī* ('Ephramean tune') is well-known to Maronite priests and church choruses.

The term *qarrādī* itself, however, cannot be elucidated in terms of the genre's relationship to the *Afrāmiyyāt*. Its etymology is interesting. Its morphology makes it a *nisba* ('relative adjective denoting descent or origin') ultimately from the noun *qird* ('monkey'). *Qarrādī* then would mean 'pertaining to or relating to *qird*'. Amīn Nakhleh, quoting his father's literary diaries,[2] suggests that the *qarrādūn* ('itinerant monkey trainers') earned their living by making their monkeys dance in village squares to the tambourine rhythms of a particular tune. This tune, according to Nakhleh, became quite popular among the villagers who then composed words to it.[3]

---

[1] See, for example, Abdel-Nour 1957, 99 and al-Jumayyil 1982, 60–61.

[2] Nakhleh 1945, 52.

[3] Nakhleh 1945, 52.

 https://doi.org/10.11647/OBP.0424.05

Whether *qarrādī* is inspired by the *Afrāmiyyāt* or by the rhythms of the monkey trainers' tambourines, music clearly is an important formal feature in the genre. The scansion of the following stanza from a well-known *Afrāmiyya*, a modern version in both *fuṣḥā* and Syriac, illustrates the adaptation that the poetic metre goes through when made to fit the musical metre:

1) *Yā ṣāliḥan ʾabdā li-l-wujūd*
–́ – ⏑ / –́ – / –́ – ⏑ / –o
'O Virtuous One who manifested to existence'

2) *Min lā shayʾin kulla mawjūd*
–́ – / –́ – / –́ ⏑ – / –́o
'From naught all that exists'

3) *Wa-ʾaqāma li-khidmatihi junūd*
⏑́ ⏑ – / ⏑́ ⏑ – / ⏑́ ⏑ ⏑ ⏑ / –́o
'And put at his service hosts'

4) *Min rūḥin wa-jismin maḥdūd*
–́ – / –́ ⏑ – / –́ – / –́o
'Of spirit and delimited body'

5) *[Ṣ]-ṣārūfīn wa-l-kārūbīn*
–́ – / –́ – / –́ – / –́o
'The Seraphim and the Cherubim'

6) *Wa-l-jullās wa-sādāt un-naʿīm*
–́ – / –́o ⏑ – / –́ – ⏑ / –́o
'And the crowds (lit. participants) and the blessed ones (in paradise?)'

7) *Wa-maṣāf un-nār bi-t-tanghīm*
⏑́ ⏑ – / –́ –o / –́ – / –́o
'And those in the fire (of hell), with tunes (and songs)'

8) *Yumajjidūnahu ʿan ḥubbin ḥamīm*
⏑́ – ⏑ – ⏑ / ⏑́ – / –́ – ⏑ / –́o
'Glorify Him out of earnest love'

9) *Ābū wi-bnu w-ruḥ qudshū*

´_ _ / ´_ _ / ´_ _ / ´_

'Father and Son and Holy Spirit'

10) *Ḥād ālūhū shārīrū*

´_ _ / ´_ _ / ´_ _ / ´_

'One true God'

Recording 6: The *Afrāmiyya* recorded by the author is at https://hdl.handle.net/20.500.12434/e18e7d75.

The number of syllables differs from one hemistich to another. There are 9 in the first, 8 in the second, 11 in the third, and 8, 7, 9, 8, 11, 7 and 7 in the rest of them. Only three hemistichs, 5, 9, and 10, have the number and quantity of syllables (7 longs) that characterise modern *qarrādī*. The stress pattern makes it clear that stresses fall on long syllables (´_), and on the first of two short syllables (ᴗ́ ᴗ), as in hemistich 8. When the lines are sung, the musical rhythm and time duration are the same in all the hemistichs. The division into feet is determined by stress boundary, in all cases moulding poetic quantity to obtain equal beat intervals. We could speak of *qarrādī*, therefore, as a stress-based metre with uniform quantity.

In order to prove that syllable number is not a formal characteristic of *qarrādī*, I made spectrograms of this *Afrāmiyya*, using a sonagraph 7029A, which was run at a 40 to 4000 hertz scale. It recorded slightly under five seconds of speech at one time. A calibration tone which had nominally 200 millisecond duration and which measured half of an inch on the spectrogram was used. After deciding where each hemistich began (the onset of the nasal resonance interval) and where its closure was, every one of the hemistichs turned out to have the exact duration of 3.2 seconds despite the significant difference in the number of syllables.

The last two hemistichs which are transliterations of a Syriac line are, like modern *qarrādī*, characterised by much more syllabic stability. This is so because Syriac exhibits the same erosion of the inflections and internal vowelling as the Lebanese dialect. One conclusion is clear. The trend in *qarrādī* has been towards more syllabic uniformity, as its modern manifestations clearly suggest. The early translations of the *Afrāmiyyāt* with their mixture of *fuṣḥā* and dialect have, in the course of the development of the genre, given way to pure dialect and consequently to poetic features influenced by the morphology and the syntax of the dialect.

The *qarrādī* piece discussed above shares a number of characteristics with the *Afrāmiyya* of Elias al-Ghazīrī, found in the Vatican Library in a manuscript written in Karshūnī and dated 1669. The whole piece is composed of twenty-two four-hemistich stanzas with the following rhyme scheme: a a a a, b b b a, c c c a, etc. For the purpose of this analysis, only the first stanza will be cited here. The transliteration is that of Jean Lecerf:[4]

1) *ʿAla smi l-ʾāb l-ʾabawiyye*
'In the name of the Father, of fatherhood'

2) *W-fī kilimto l-ʾazaliyye*
'And His eternal Word'

3) *W-rūḥ quduso fi s-sawiyye*
'And his equal Holy Spirit'

---

[4] The entire poem is cited by Whaybeh 1952, 145–48. The four lines studied here are quoted by LeCerf 1932, 240.

4) *(ʾU)rattib abyāt ʾEfremiyye*
'I compose the lines of an *Afrāmiyya*'

Sung to the *qarrādī* tune the following stress pattern emerges:

1) ⏑ / –́ – / –́ – / ⏑́ ⏑ – / –́ 9 syllables
2) / –́ ⏑ / –́ – / ⏑́ ⏑ – / –́ 8 syllables
3) / –́ ⏑ ⏑ / ⏑́ – / ⏑́ – / –́ 8 syllables
4) ⏑ / –́ – – / –́o – / –́ – / –́ 9 syllables

Assuming that Lecerf's reading is correct, we have a *qarrādī* with an uneven number of syllables but which, nevertheless, fits the musical metre showing a pattern of rhythm similar to the *Afrāmiyya* cited above.

In the more modern *qarrādī*, short syllables become rather rare, although by no means absent. Occasionally, depending on their position in the hemistich, they even receive the stress. The examples below are taken from popular village rhymes called *ʿaddiyyāt*[5] ('counting rhymes'), and they are cited here to show a few of the many syllabic characteristics of *qarrādī* as well as the more popular rhyme schemes:

A. a) *Taʿū nimshi nʿid d-ibyāt*
⏑́ – / –́ – / –́ – / –́o
'Come let us walk and count rhymes'

a^{i}) *ʿAlā shaykh[i] libsaynāt*
⏑́ – / –́ – / –́ – / –́o
'About the sheikh of cats'

[5] In Lebanese folklore, these *ʿaddiyyāt* are 'counting rhymes' sung to infants and little children by their mothers before they go to bed or to lull them into sleep. A collection of *ʿaddiyyāt* is cited in Frayḥa 1957, 207–25.

b) *ʿA*[6] *khibzātī ribbaytu*[7]
ᴗ́ _ / _́ _ / _́ _ / ᴗ́
'I bred him on my on my own bread'

b$^{i)}$ *ʾĀkal lī*[8] *kill il-jibnāt*
ᴗ́ _ / _́ _ / _́ _ / _́o
'(But) he ate all the cheese (my cheese)'

c) *Imt-i ḥmiltu-w-waʾ-ʾaʿtu*
_́ _ / _́ _ / _́ _ / ᴗ́
'So I carried him, (having) caught him in the act'

c^{i}) *ʿInd il-ʾāḍī shāraʿtu*
_́ _ / _́ _ / _́ _ / ᴗ́
'At the judge's place, I argued with him (the judge)'

d) *Ṭaylaʿ lī ʾarbaʿ fatwāt*
. _́ _ / _́ _ / _́ _ / _́o
'(And so) he gave me four legal opinions'

Rhyme scheme: a a, b a, b b, a, etc.

B. a) *Yā ʿaskar ʾum iskar*[9]
_́ _ / _́ p / _́ _ / _́
'Hey soldiers, get up and get drunk!'

a^{i}) *[W]-khabbī lī ʾālib sukkar*[10]
_́ _ / _́ _ / _́ _ / _́
'And save for me a piece of sugar'

b) *Dallitnī sittī ʿa l-bīr*
_́ _ / _́ _ / _́ _ / _́o
'My grandmother showed me where the well is'

---

[6] *ʿa* and *ʿā* are both used in different melodies.

[7] At the end of the line, the last syllable is often lengthened.

[8] *Akallī* and *ākallī* are rendered as such in different melodies.

[9] Frayḥa 1957, 209.

[10] *Sukkar* may be rendered as *sukkār* in particular melodies.

b^{i}) *[W]-jābit lī   shanbar ḥarīr*
–́ – / –́ – / –́ ⏓ / –́o
'And she brought me a silk scarf'

c) *ʾIlti   llā ya*[11] *sitti mn ayn*
–́ – / –́ ⏓ / –́ – / –́o
'I said to her, "Where did you get it from, Grandma?"'

c^{i}) *ʾĀlit   lī min ʿind il-mīr*
–́ – / –́ – / –́ – / –́o
'"From the Mayor's house," she said'

Rhyme scheme: a a, b b, c b, etc.

Hemistich a above presents an interesting case of compensation. It contains six syllables, one of which, number 3, is succeeded by a pause to compensate for the lost syllable. Occasionally in cases such as this one, instead of a pause, a nonsensical syllable like *iw* is inserted to make up for lost time duration. This is a further indication that every foot in *qarrādī* has an abstract quantity roughly equal to that of each of the other feet in the hemistich.

C. a) *Yā ḥādī [w]-yā māḍī*[12]
–́ – / –́ p / –́ – / –́
'O singer of *ḥidā*, O travelling one!'

a^{i}) *Mallī   jrābak ziwwādī*
–́ – / –́ – / ´ – / –́
'Fill your bag with provisions'

b) *[N]-kannak ʿa blādī ghādī*
–́ – / –́ – / –́ – / –́
'If you are going to my country'

---

[11] The vocative *yā* is usually a long syllable, but in the vernacular, it is often shortened to *ya*.

[12] Frayḥa 1957, 210.

b^{i}) *Baladī [i]-blād ish-shām*
ᴗ́ ᴗ _́ / p _́ / _ _ / _́o
'My country is Syria'

c) *Fīha l-khawkh wi-r-rimmān*
_́ _ / _́ p / _́ _ / _́o
'There are in it (Syria) plums and pomegranates'

c^{i}) *Fīha skaykit il-ʿasfūr*
_́ _ / _́ _ / _́ _ / _́o
'There are in it bird perches'

d) *Fīha sh-shaykhi blā ṭanṭūr*
_́ _ / _́ _ / _́ _ / _́o
'There are in it sheikhs without headdress'

d^{i}) *Ṭanṭūrak ʿallā ʿallā*
_́ _ / _́ _ / _́ _ / _́
'Your headdress flew up on high'

e) *Ghaṭṭ[i] ʿā ḥayt il-Mullā*
_́ ᴗ / _́ _ / _́ _ / _́
'It alighted on the mullah's wall'

e^{i}) *Shāf il-ḥamā titfallā*
_́ _ / ᴗ́ _ / _́ _ / _́
'(And) saw the mother-in-law searching her hair for lice'

f) *[W]-ʾamlithā haṭ-ṭūl*
_́ _ / _́ _ / _́o
'And her louse is very big'

Rhyme scheme: a a, a b, c d, d e, e e, f

In this example, in addition to the pause in c, which is also rendered as: *Fīha l-khawkh[i] wi-r-rimmān* by inserting the vowel *i*, we have in b^{i} a case where two syllables constitute a foot. These two syllables, though shorter than the rest in the hemistich are slightly lengthened (especially the first one which bears the stress) in order to conform to the musical metre. Hemistich f is two syllables shorter than the rest, but it has the same pattern of stress and is, therefore, considered here as a shorter form of *qarrādī*. The appearance of short hemistichs at the conclusion of a *qarrādī* stanza is quite frequent, and one reason for their appearance may be a closured technique connected with the ending of one stanza and the beginning of another.

C.[13] g) *Yā ḥādī wi-ḥdī lhā*
–́ – / –́ – / –́o / –́
'O singer of *ḥidā*, sing (*ḥidā*) for her'

g[i]) *Il-wardi b-mandīlhā*
–́ – / –́ – / –́o / –́
'There are roses in her scarf'

h) *[W]-yā bayyā waddī lhā*
–́ – / –́ – / –́o / –́
'And O her father, send to her'

h[i]) *Sabʿ itman dihbāt ikbār*
–́ – / –́ – / –́o / – –́o
'Seven or eight pieces of gold'

i) *Tat ḥiṭṭun bi-srīrhā*
–́ – / –́ – / –́o / –́
'So that she'd put them on her bed'

j) *Yā ḥādī wi-ḥdī daghshī*
–́ – / –́ – / –́ – / –́
'O singer of *ḥidā*, sing *ḥidā* at night (or late evening)'

j[i]) *Rakkib Laylā*[14] *ʿal jaḥshī*
–́ – / –́ – / –́ – / –́
'Help Layla mount on the donkey'

---

[13] Continued.

[14] The second syllable in *Laylā* is slightly shortened to accommodate the stress on the first syllable.

k) *Rakkibhā [w]-sir fīhā*
´– – / ´– p / ´– – / ´–
'Help her mount and help her along'

k^{i}) *[Iw]-dir bālak tirmīhā*
´– – / ´– – / ´– – / ´–
'Make sure you don't let her fall'

l) *Byiʿmillak bayyā balshī*
´– – / ´– – / ´– – / ´–
'Her father will give you trouble'

Again, here the singer of *qarrādī* may use a pause in the place of a syllable or may in each case insert an *i* vowel (or, in some cases an *iw* instead of a silent *wāw*) instead of the pause: *ḥdī l[i]hā*, *mandīl[i]hā*, *waddī l[i]hā*, *srīr[i]hā*. Occasionally, an extra-long syllable in the middle of the hemistich is shortened in order to make it conform to the rhythm, as, for example, in the two imperative verbs *sīr* and *dīr* above.[15]

Finally, the following line from a popular *ʿaddiyya* shows the first hemistich composed of five syllables with two pauses, while the second one has eight syllables, seven long and one short[16] in fourth position:

a) *Ḥū ḥū yā bardī*
´– p / ´– p / ´– – / ´–
'Brrr, brrr, I'm freezing'

a^{i}) *Ash ʾūshit ḥaṭab mā ʿindī*
[_][17] ´– – ˘́ – – – –
'I don't even have a piece of kindling wood'

[15] *Sīr* and *dīr* are the actual vernacular pronunciations of the *fuṣḥā* imperatives, *sir* and *dur*. This preference for the *fuṣḥā* forms is dictated by the musical meter.

[16] This short syllable is given roughly the same quantity as the rest.

[17] Here the first syllable is hardly heard. On compensation, see below.

The pervasive nature of the *qarrādī* genre, its presence in the folk poetry of Lebanon, Syria, Palestine and Iraq, to mention only a few countries with living folk traditions, makes its derivation solely from Maronite Church homilies and hymns less likely. It is more probable that the genre predates the *Afrāmiyyāt* and is as old as the Arabic language itself. The following lines from an old Shiʿite hymn testify to the genre's prevalence in Islamic material:

> *ʿAlī Ḥaydar il-karrār*
> ᴗ́ – –́ ᴗ –́ – –́o
> "ʿAlī Ḥaydar,[18] the great warrior'
>
> *ʾĀsim il-janni wi-n-nār*
> –́ ᴗ –́ – ᴗ́ – –́o
> '(The one) who has severed Heaven from Hell'
>
> *Shifiʿ ʿalā ʾimmitu*
> ᴗ́ – ᴗ́ – –́ ᴗ –́
> '(He) has interceded on behalf of his people'
>
> *Yawm il-ʿaṭash il-ʾakbar*
> –́ – ᴗ́ ᴗ –́ – –́o
> 'On the day of the Great Thirst (Doomsday)'

Another indication of *qarrādī*'s ancient origin comes from the Muslim's chanting to the *qarrādī* tune, of the first of the Five Pillars of Islam, that of the profession of faith (*shahada*):

> *Lā ilāha illa l-Lāh*
> –́ ᴗ –́ ᴗ –́ – –́o
> 'There is no god but Allah (God)'
>
> *Muḥammad Rasūla l-Lāh*
> ᴗ́ – –́ ᴗ –́ – –́o
> 'Muḥammad is the messenger of Allah'

[18] ʿAlī Ḥaydar is the fourth caliph of Islam.

It is to be noted that even in this *fuṣḥā* example the morphology of words is compromised to suit the musical metre and that the first short syllable in the second hemistich, which coincides with the first musical accent, receives the stress.

The examples above show that *qarrādī* is neither, strictly speaking, a syllabic, nor an accentual syllabic, nor a quantitative metre. The number and quantity of syllables vary from one line to another. Within each *qarrādī* composition, every line is sung in exactly the same time as that of each of the other lines, variations in melody notwithstanding. The regular pattern of stress obtained is the most important formal feature of *qarrādī*. Natural stress and poetic stress are constantly suppressed in favour of a superimposed musical accentual pattern.

The fact that such a musical pattern is prevalent in a large number of syntactically and morphologically unrelated languages, further indicates that the metre of *qarrādī* lies outside the poetic, metrical structure of any one of these languages. The following 'comptines' ('counting rhymes') and children's rhymes from Hebrew, French, English, German, Danish, Greek and Russian point to the universality of *qarrādī*'s rhythmic pattern:[19]

HEBREW	Transliteration
בוֹא אֱלַי פַּרְפַּר נֶחְמָד	Bó elaí parpár nechmád
שֵׁב אֶצְלִי עַל כַּף הַיָּד	Schév etzlí al káf hayád
שֵׁב, תָּנוּחַ, אַל תִּירָא	Schév tanúach ál tirá
וְתָעוּף בַּחֲזָרָה	Vé teúf becházará

[19] The following 'comptines' and popular melodies were solicited from colleagues in the various language departments at the University of Massachusetts, Amherst.

Translation

Come to me, nice butterfly
Sit on my palm
Sit, rest, don't be afraid
And you'll fly back again

FRENCH	Translation
Úne póule súr un múr	A chicken on a wall
Qúi picóte dú pain dúr	That pecks dry bread
Pícotí pícotá	Peck peck peck
Lá voilá quí s'en vá	Let's see who will go

ENGLISH

Éeny, méeny, míny, mó
Cátch a tíger bý the tóe,
Íf he hóllers, lét him gó, Éeny,
méeny, míny, mó

GERMAN	Translation
Ích, und, dú und Béckers kúh	I and you and Becker's cow
Mű́ller ésel-dér bist dú	Müller's jackass that is you

DANISH	Translation
Lílle kónge kón nu frém	Little king, come forth now
Éllers gǻr vi áldrig hjém	Or we won't go home

GREEK	Transliteration
Ἔλα πᾶμε ὀδηγέ	Éla páme ódhigé
Γιά νά τούς περάσουμε	Ghía ná tous perásoumé
Καί νά σέ κεράσουμε	Kaí na sé kerásoumé

Translation

Come on, driver
Let's pass them (cars)
And let us treat you to (name of pastry)

I have talked briefly about compensation. Since the musical metre of *qarrādī* is so pervasive in popular Lebanese songs, I shall choose three popular Lebanese tunes, discuss the effect of musical metre on syllable quality and quantity, and elucidate further the role of compensation. The three tunes are *Layyā w-layyā*, *ʿAl-yādī* and *Ya-ghzayyil*, respectively:[20]

Figure 8: The three tunes

Recording 7: A recording of *Layyā w-layyā* by the author is found at https://hdl.handle.net/20.500.12434/b4a6b4ea.

[20] These tunes were sung by Dr Mansour Ajami and transcribed in musical notations by Lois al-Faruqi. Note that the macron > below is used to distinguish musical accent from poetic stress, indicated by ´ over the particular syllables.

First, *Layyā w-layyā*:

> *Layya w-layyā w-ya bnayyā*
> — — — — p — — —
> 'Layya, Layya![21] O little (daughter)'
>
> *Ya Layla l-badawiyyā*
> ᴗ — — ᴗ ᴗ — —
> 'O Bedouin Layla!'

In the first hemistich, the poetic scansion shows a seven-syllable *qarrādī* line. When read without reference to music, the second hemistich scans with three short syllables. Yet when the musical metre is superimposed upon the poetic one, the musical accent locates the stress in the poetic line:

	Lay yaw lay yā	*yab nay yā*
	ᴗ > ᴗ ᴗ > ᴗ ᴗ >	>
music	ᴗ — ᴗ ᴗ — ᴗ ᴗ —	— —
poetry	— — — —	— — —

Here the musical accents are on the second, fourth, sixth and eighth beats. Since musical accent is the key to poetic stress, the stressed poetic syllables will be the second, the fourth, the fifth and the seventh: — —́ — —́ p —́ — —́.

Taking the pause after the fourth syllable into consideration, we seem to have an iambic stress pattern rather than the usual trochaic one associated with *qarrādī*. What is happening here is that the hemistich starts on an offbeat and the music compensates by introducing an extra beat after the fourth poetic syllable (i.e., the fifth musical note *yā* was held over) in order to produce a "trochaic" pattern of stress. Thus:

[21] *Layya* is an uncommon proper name repeated in all the *Layyā w-Layyā* genre.

music ⏑ –̆> ...

Counting from syllable two on, in the poetic hemistich, we have in reality seven syllables in the familiar stress pattern of *qarrādī*. The second hemistich gives the same picture, again starting on an offbeat and holding over *bā* and its musical counterpart.

Compensation in *ʿAl-yādī* takes place in a similar fashion but with the difference that both hemistichs do not start on an offbeat and the held-over syllables are the last note in the first hemistich and the penultimate and final poetic syllables of the second hemistich (second hemistich, second measure).

ʿAl yā dil yā dil yā dī

music –̂ – –̂ – –̂ – –̂ (held over for two longs)

poetry –́ – –́ – –́ – –́ [–] (no poetic syllable)

Yam mī liʿ bay diy *yā*

music –̂ – –̂ – –̂ (held over) –̂ (held over)

poetry –́ – –́ – –́ [–] –́ [–] (no poetic syllables)

Recording 8: A recording by the author can be found at https://hdl.handle.net/20.500.12434/ae9b02ae.

Taking into account the musical stress pattern, we can understand the apparently anomalous pattern of poetic stress: –́ – –́ – –́ –́ where the last two syllables receive the stress without an intervening unstressed syllable. It bears repeating that reference to poetic scansion alone is not a sure indication of syllable number or quality.

Ya-ghzayyil presents yet another example of compensation:

ya gh zay yil yā bū-l-ḥay bā
music ^ ^ > > >
— — — — — — — —
yagh zay yil yā bū-l-ḥay bā
poetry ´ ´ ´ ´
— — — — — — —
'Little ghazal, possessed of beauty'

mar ḥab tayn ū mar ḥay bā
music > > > >
— — — — — — —
mar ḥab tayn uw mar ḥay bā
poetry ´ ´ ´ ´
— — — — — — —
'Hello twice and once more'

Recording 9: A recording by the author is found at https://hdl.handle.net/20.500.12434/86c6f703.

Here the last poetic syllable, normally stressed in *qarrādī*, receives no stress. By holding over poetic syllable #5 for the time of two syllables as in *ʿAl-yādī*, the musical metre has, as it were, implied an extra poetic syllable that does not actually exist (corresponding to the eighth musical syllable). Stress location, therefore, not syllable number, is essential in delineating the poetic formal characteristics of this tune and the various other manifestations of a *qarrādī* line.

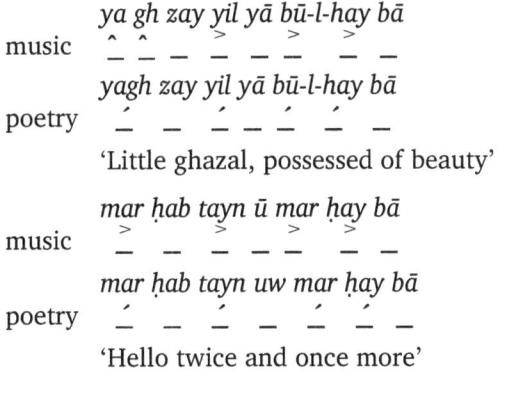

So far we have seen that musical metre can accommodate as many as eleven syllables (no more than eight of which can be long poetic syllables) or as few as six in a four-accent segment. Compensation, either by shortening or lengthening syllables is, however, restricted. Two conditions seem to be necessary: conformity to a duple rhythm and a recurring hemistich time duration. Nine long syllables, I have observed, cannot be suited to the *qarrādī* tune, and they are usually rendered musically in a 'dactylic' pattern of stress when the hemistichs are scanned in alternation. The following lines from a famous song by Wadīʿ al-Ṣāfī, one of Lebanon's famous singers, serves as an illustration:

(a) *Bi-s-sāḥat lāʾaynā bi-s-sāḥa*
– –́ – – –́ – – –́ ᴗ[22]
'In the courtyard we met, in the courtyard'

(a^{i}) *[ʿ]layhā jawzi ʿyūn shū dabbāḥā*
– –́ – – –́o – – –́ –
'She has a couple of eyes'

(b) *[W]-ʾāmī yikhz il-ʿayn w-il-khaddayni*
– –́ – – –́o – – –́ –
'And a figure, may the evil eye be kept away, and two cheeks'

(b^{i}) *Tiffāḥā bitghār min tiffāḥā*
– –́ – – –́o – – –́ –
'An apple jealous of another apple'

Stress pattern: – –́ – –́ – – –́ – – // – –́ – – –́ – – –́ –

The recorded examples show that Lebanese *zajal* does not utilise ten long-syllable hemistichs or lines, though combinations of seven and four are quite popular. These appear in a kind of strophic poem often referred to as a *muwashshaḥa* because of its similarity to the Spanish poem of the same name. Although the lines in these poems are declaimed or sung without caesura, they are clearly demarcated by their rhyme patterns. In some parts of Lebanon, this genre is referred to as *huzām* or *khuzām*,[23] but it is also called *maʿannā muwashshaḥ* by some critics.[24] This is also a stress-based metre that resembles the shorter *qarrādī* in musical

22 Note that the last syllable is shorter than the rest.

23 For example, in the Kisirwān and the Biqāʿ region in eastern Lebanon.

24 See, for example, Whaybeh 1952, 65–66.

durations and shows a close correlation between poetic syllables and musical durations. In the example below two musical durations are used: 16th notes and 8th notes. The latter are consistently used to accompany long poetic syllables while each 16th note sets either a short syllable or is used in pairs to set a long syllable. In other words, syllable length is roughly equivalent to musical duration in this *zajal* genre. In the musical transcription that follows,[25] musical accent appears on every other 8th beat, and this appears to be the case in all the poems studied.

Figure 9: *Huzām/khuzām*

Recording 10: A recording by the author can be accessed at https://hdl.handle.net/20.500.12434/29ac227a.

The musical accentual pattern can be best described as irregular in that the corresponding poetic stress alternates an 'iambic' with a 'trochaic' pattern. Thus, the twelve musical syllables (corresponding to 11 poetic syllables) are accented as follows:

 \>   \>   \>   \>   \>   \>
_ _ _ _ _ _ _ _ _ _ _ _ _ line one
\>   \>   \>   \>   \>   \>
_ _ _ _ _ _ _ _ _ _ _ _ _ line two

or, the following pattern of stress obtains in the poetic lines:

[25] This is a popular anonymous *muwashshaḥa* familiar to afficionados of *zajal*.

[m]ḍayyaᶜ ʾalbi w-ashwāʾū   *ᶜal lī ma shtāʾ*
– –́ – –́ – –́ –   –́ – –́ –
[w]-kill illī ḥabbū fāʾū   *[w]-ʾalbī mā fāʾ*
–́ – –́ – –́ – –́   – –́ – –́

The typical *khuzām* poem consists of a couplet and a number of quatrains ranging from four to twenty or more. The couplet is repeated after each quatrain, thus bringing back the rhyme of the framing couplet. In addition to that, every second line in every quatrain is itself repeated to emphasise the rhyme of the particular quatrain as a whole. The following poem will clarify these stress and rhyme relationships:

Refrain

Fāyʾā shū laᶜabtīnā   *bi-l basket ball*
– –́ – –́ – –́ –   –́ – –́ –
'Do you remember how often we played'   'with the basketball'
[W]-yā ma w-yā ma nṭartīnā   *derrière l'école*
–́ – –́ –   –́ – –́   – –́ – –́
'And how often you waited for us'   'behind the school?'

Quatrain #1

Niḥna ᶜshiʾna w-ḥabbaynā   *dans une rencontre*
– –́ – –́   – –́ –   –́ – –́ –
'We fell in love'   'during a meeting between us'
[W]-lamma rjiᶜnā tlāʾaynā   *[m]shīnā ᶜal-montre*
–́ – –́ – –́ – –́   – –́ – –́
'And when we met again'   'we met regularly (as though we kept time)'
[W]-biḥyātik shū sawwaynā   *Avec les autres*
– –́ – –́ – –́ –   –́ – –́ –
'And by your life, what did we do'   'to the others?'
(i.e., how could we have angered the others?)

Tā ḥattā ḥaṭṭu ʿlaynā	*kill hal contrôle*
‘That they have imposed upon us’	‘all these restrictions’

Quatrain #2

Min ḥisnik min alṭāfik	*j’aime la lecture*
‘Because of your beauty and kindness’	‘I love the reading’
[W]-ʾalbī awwal mā shāfik	*allī bien-sûr*
‘And when my heart first saw you’	‘it said to me, “Of course.”’
[W]-lawlā shāfū awṣāfik	*et ta figure*
‘And if they [people] saw your physical traits’	‘and your face’
Kānu khtarʿu-m nishfāfik	*tous les alcools*
‘They would have invented from your lips’	‘all of alcohol (hard liquor)’

Quatrain #3

ʿAm biḥki b-fiʿl il-māḍī	*pour décider*
‘I am using the past tense’	‘in order to decide’
Jāfaytīni w-ʿal fāḍī	*tu m’a grondé*
‘You have become estranged from me and for no reason’	‘you scolded me’
Rāsi mn il-ḥibb il-māḍī	*a eu d’idées*
‘Because of past love, my head’	‘had ideas’
[W]-niyyālik rāsik fāḍī	*comme une casserole*
‘How fortunate you are! Your head is empty’	‘like a pot’

Quatrain #4

Mashyithā na'lī na'lī	*dans le marché*
– –́– –́– –́–	–́ – –́–
'She walks a step at a time'	'in the marketplace'
[W]-ḥayth iktīr ib-tilba' lī	*je ne peux changer*
–́ – –́ ––́––́	– –́ – –́
'And because she becomes me well'	'I don't want to change'
[W]-ma byikfī ikhdit 'a'lī	*[w] tous mes objects*
– –́– –́– –́–	–́ – –́–
'And as though it wasn't enough that she took my mind'	'and all my objects'
Ṣar badhā tirkab sha'lī	*sur mes épaules*
–́ ––́––́ ––́	– –́ – –́
'Now she wants to take a ride'	'on my shoulders'

Rhyme scheme:

	___a	___b	refrain
	___a	___b	
	___c	___d	
	___c	___d	
chorus repeats	(___c	___d)	quatrain #1
	___c	___d	
	___c	___b	
chorus repeats	(___a	___b)	
	(___a	___b)	
	___e	___f	
	___e	___f	
chorus repeats	(___e	___f)	
	___e	___f	quatrain #2
	___e	___b	
chorus repeats	(___a	___b)	
	(___a	___b)	etc.

Stress pattern:

iambic	___a	___b	refrain
trochaic	___a	___b	
iambic	___c	___d	

trochaic	___c	___d	
trochaic	___c	___d	(chorus)
iambic	___c	___d	
trochaic	___c	___d	
iambic	___a	___b	refrain
trochaic	___a	___b	etc.

This most interesting anonymous *muwashshaḥa* employs both Arabic and French in a fashion reminiscent of some Hispano-Arabic prototypes. It was chosen as an example of *khuzām* in order to demonstrate the facility with which these two languages, whose metrics and rhythms are significantly different, can be used interchangeably without deference to their particular metrical characteristics. What makes this possible is precisely the fact that neither of them is used to produce a semblance of either Arabic or French rhythms. We are dealing here with a musical metre which imposes on the two languages its own rhythms, despite the obvious slighting of some of the vocalised syllables. It is true that *zajal* poets occasionally insert a foreign word in a verse of *maʿannā*, as in the following:[26]

Hal ḥilwit illī shiftihā fī ghayr[i] hall
_ _ ᴗ _ / _ _ ᴗ _ / _ _ ᴗ _ /
'This beautiful woman that I saw in a different hall'

Ḥaṭṭū ma bayni w-baynihā malyūn[i] wall
_ _ ᴗ _ / _ _ ᴗ _ / _ _ ᴗ _ /
'They (people) placed between us a million walls'

Such words are always one-syllable rhyme words, which do not seem to affect the rhythm or syllable pattern. In *khuzām*, on the

---

[26] The two hemistichs are by Zaghlūl al-Dāmūr, improvised in one of his *zajal* contests in Detroit, Michigan in 1974.

other hand, whole hemistichs or whole lines may be in a different language since the music in this case determines the rhythm of the poetic line.

* * *

Another *naẓm* metre is that of the popular folk tune *dalʿūnā* which typically starts with the refrain a a. The rhyme a always consists of *nā*, the last syllable of the word *dalʿūnā*. The most frequently used refrain is

> *ʿĀ lā dalʿūnā [w]-ʿa lā dalʿūnā*
>
> — — — — —   — — — — —
>
> '(Sing) to the tune of *dalʿūnā*. (Sing) to the tune of *dalʿūnā*'
>
> *Rāḥu l-ḥabāyib mā waddaʿūnā*
>
> — — ᴗ — — — — ᴗ — —
>
> 'The loved ones left; they did not say goodbye to us'

followed by strophes rhyming b b b a, c c c a, d d d a, etc. There are two related melodies, the *Biqāʿī*[27] and the *Bayrūtī*:[28]

Figure 10: *Biqāʿī*

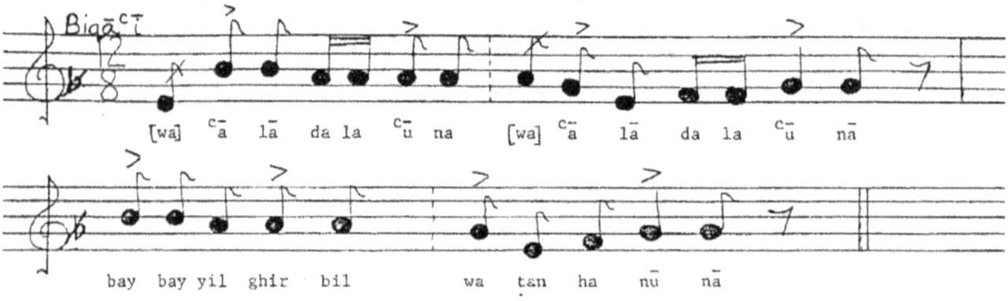

Recording 11: A recording of the *Biqāʿī* by the author can be accessed at https://hdl.handle.net/20.500.12434/135ea560.

[27] *Biqāʿī* refers to the Biqāʿ region in eastern Lebanon. The two hemistichs translate as follows: 'Sing to the tune of *dalʿūna*; sing to the tune of *dalʿūna* / Damn the life in estrangement; the homeland is always in the heart'.

[28] *Bayrūtī* refers to a particular melody of *dalʿūna* popularised in Beirut.

Figure 11: *Bayrūtī*

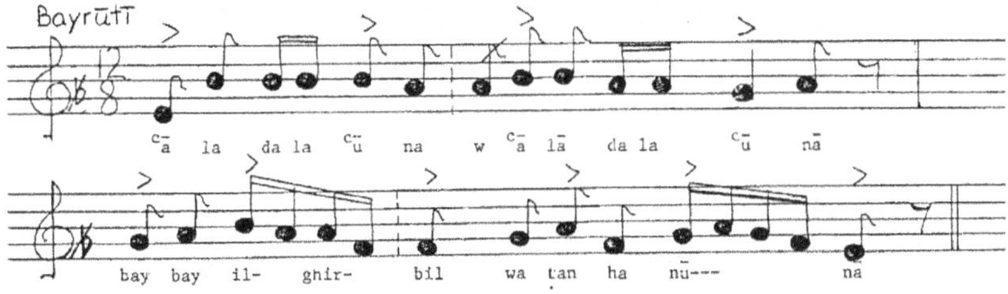

Recording 12: A recording of the *Bayrūtī* by the author can be found at https://hdl.handle.net/20.500.12434/bb37e5cd.

The *Biqāʿī* has a stress pattern consisting of a dactyl and a trochee, ´_ _ _ ´_ _ in each hemistich. Thus the hemistich divides at stress boundary into two parts: ´_ _ _ and ´_ _. As we mentioned above, Abdel-Nour assumes that *dalʿūnā* divides quantitatively into _ _ / _ _ _, repeated twice.[29] He gives no justification for that arbitrary division or for his assumption that the metre is a quantitative one. The musical transcription gives ample proof that the metre of *dalʿūnā*, especially in the *Biqāʿī* version, is a stress-based metre rendered in a rhythm unlike anything recorded by al-Khalīl. The *Bayrūtī* melody starts off with the same stress pattern as that of the *Biqāʿī* and continues in every odd line in the piece. All even lines revert to a duple measure with the familiar trochaic pattern, even at the expense of distorting natural stress and pronunciation of some words.

Unlike *qarrādī* in which there is fluctuation in syllable number and syllable quantity, *dalʿūnā* is characterised by five long syllables, admitting occasionally a short one which is lengthened to preserve the foot division. The appearance of a short syllable

[29] See Abdel-Nour 1957, 106.

in the third position (–́ – ⏑ –́ –) is more frequent than in the first (⏑́ – – –́ –) or in the fourth (–́ – – ⏑́ –). Short syllables in the second and fifth positions are rare.

6. *ʿATĀBĀ*, *MĪJANĀ*, AND OTHER POPULAR GENRES

Writing in 1932, Jean Lecerf observed that *ʿatābā* was a modern genre of great popularity among the poets of the time, and that *mījanā* "ne parait pas constituer autre chose qu'une variété de *ʿatābā*" ('does not appear to constitute anything other than a variety of *ʿatābā*').[1] While the popularity of both genres is still much in evidence throughout the villages of Lebanon, they are recognised by critics as belonging to two distinct Khalilian metres, *rajaz* in the case of *mījanā* and a form of *wāfir* in the case of *ʿatābā*.

Part of the difficulty of distinguishing these two genres from each other lies, I believe, in the similarity of their improvisatory *nathr* style and in the fact that a *mījanā* refrain introduces and concludes every *ʿatābā* verse. When a poet is asked to sing a *bayt* of *ʿatābā* (a *bayt*, 'verse', is composed of four hemistichs), he starts with the popular *mījanā* hemistich which consists of singing *yā mījanā* three times followed by another hemistich with the same rhyme. The second hemistich then becomes a refrain which the chorus repeats twice at the end of every *ʿatābā* verse. The poet moves smoothly from *mījanā* to *ʿatābā* by interposing an *owf* (lit. a sign of tedium, exasperation or ennui) between the *mījanā* hemistichs and the ensuing *ʿatābā* verse. This syllable allows a sort of coloratura, or a virtuoso display of the voice. A similar display takes place at the end of the *ʿatābā* verse, as though to

[1] Lecerf 1952, 179–258.

 https://doi.org/10.11647/OBP.0424.06

cue in the chorus for their rendering and repetition of the second *mījanā* hemistich.

If the poet wishes, however, to sing the *mījanā* verse himself, he often does so without recourse to the *owf*. This is an important feature which helps the listener identify the two genres and understand how they relate to and how they differ from each other.

The refrain-like *mījanā* plays an important role in giving the poet time to compose his next *bayt* of *ʿatābā*. The verse of *mījanā* is often called *kasrit mījanā* because it implies this time factor. In the Lebanese dialect, *kasara lahu* is pronounced *kasarlu* and means 'he prepared the way for him', that is, to give enough time for improvisation.

Strictly speaking, therefore, it is incorrect to consider *mījanā* as a variety of *ʿatābā*, as Lecerf does. Numerous printed works include verbal duels in both *ʿatābā* and *mījanā*. One poet might start with a *bayt* of *ʿatābā*, and the other would answer with a *mījanā* verse and so one until the end of the duel. If there is no chorus, which happens occasionally, the poets often make the transition between the two genres with the *owf*.

In terms of structure the two genres exhibit some similarities in their rhyme schemes. The typical *ʿatābā* verse contains three homonyms, one at the end of each of the first three hemistichs, and a compulsory rhyme at the end of the fourth that ends most commonly with *āb* or *ab*, sometimes with *ār*, sometimes with *ā* without a final consonant, and less frequently with *ī*. Consider the following *bayt*:

Khidīnī b-ʿaṯfiki w-ḥilmik wi-ʿadlik
'Treat me with your love, your patience and your justice'

Ta ḥatta n ghibit irjaʿ lik wa-ʿud lik
'So that if I went away, I would return and come back to you'

Ḥalaft illik bijī w-ʾalbī wa-ʿadlik
'I swore to you I would come and my heart made you a promise'

Waʿid zaghlūl[2] *mish mawʿidi ghrāb*
'The promise of a songbird, not the promise of a crow'

In this *bayt*, the play on words is affected by the use of the conjunction *wa* with *ʿadl* ('justice') and *ʿud* ('to return', from the verb *ʿāda*, imperfect, *yaʿūdu)* in the first two hemistichs, and with *waʿada* ('to promise') in the third hemistich. The fourth hemistich ends with *-āb*, as in the majority of *ʿatābā* verses.[3]

Likewise, most *mījanā* verses employ three homonyms but the fourth hemistich must close with a word ending with *nā*, as in the following example:[4]

ʾĀlū btihwa s-simir ʾiltillun balā
'They asked, "Do you love brunettes?" I said, "Yes."'

Wish shiʾir minhun ma byijī ʾilla l-balā
'Nothing comes out of blondes except disaster'

[Iw]-shū nafiʿ kill li-l-ʿimir wi-d-dinyī balā
'What's the use of (this) life and (this) world without'

Shiʾr iw-simir khallu l-ḥakī baynātinā
'Brunettes and blondes; let's keep these words between us'

---

[2] This *bayt* is attributed to the great *zajal* poet Zaghlūl al-Dāmūr.

[3] Another possible ending for an *ʿatābā* verse is *-ār*.

[4] The following *bayt* of *mījanā* is by Zaghlūl al-Dāmūr in one well-known verbal duel.

Here the homonyms *balā* ('yes' in *fuṣḥā*), *balā* ('disaster') and *balā* ('without') constitute the rhyme in the first three hemistichs. The rhyme *-nā* in the fourth hemistich returns to the end rhyme in the principal *mījanā* hemistich (*yā mījanā yā mījanā yā mījanā*), which presages the main verses or strophes that follow. Neither Whaybeh nor Nakhleh mention the use of homonyms in *mījanā*, which does not seem to agree with the available data.[5] Both writers use examples from written works in which the first three hemistichs of the *mījanā* verse have a common rhyme but are not homonyms, and in which the fourth hemistich ends with a *-nā* rhyme. Such a rhyme scheme does exist, though it is less frequent in improvised *mījanās* and verbal duels. On the other hand, rhyme in *ʿatābā* is always based on homonyms.

The use of homonyms seems to predate the earliest recorded Lebanese *zajals*. These are as old as Arabic poetry itself and most probably in direct development from an old genre of *fuṣḥā* poetry known as the *muthallathāt* (the 'threesomes', or the 'three homonyms'), about which little has been written.[6] Perhaps the most famous collection of such poems is the *Muthallathāt of Quṭrub* (d. 821) published and edited by Edvardus Vilmar in 1856. This is a critical edition in Latin which discusses, among other things, the metre and form of the *Muthallathāt*. In 1914 the same collection, along with a poetic commentary employing the same homonymous rhymes, was edited and published by Louis

[5] See Whaybeh 1952, 78 and Nakhleh 1945, 39–45.

[6] The author is not aware of any thorough modern study of the *muthallath* genre in the *fuṣḥā* tradition.

Cheikho in *al-Bulgha fī shudhūr al-lugha.*[7] The metre used in these *muthallathāt* is a short *rajaz* consisting of two rather than three feet and exhibiting the well-known syllabic licences. It often takes the following two forms: _ _ ᴗ _ / ᴗ _ _ and _ _ ᴗ _ / _ _ _.

The metre employed by the commentator has the following syllabic configuration: _ _ ᴗ _ / _ _ ᴗ _ / _ _ _ or _ _ ᴗ _ / _ _ ᴗ _ / ᴗ _ _. The first radical in the first homonym in both the *Muthallathāt* of Quṭrub and those of the commentator is vowelled with a *fatḥa*. The second and the third are vowelled with *kasra* and *ḍamma* respectively. Every one of Quṭrub's fourth hemistichs ends with the rhyme letter *bāʾ*, preceded by a consonant with a short vowel, while those of the commentator always end with a consonant *rāʾ* after a long *ā*.

While *ʿatābā* and *mījanā* do not follow this method closely, the formal similarities that exist between them and the *muthallathāt* clearly suggest a continuum in the development of the genre, an adaptation in the vernacular of a rhyme scheme which is predicated upon wordplay and verbal virtuosity. At times, *zajal* poets compose two hemistichs, selecting two difficult homonyms, and then challenge other poets to supply the third to finish the *bayt*. The challenge is usually taken seriously since failure to meet it would cast serious doubt on a poet's reputation. The difficulty can be insurmountable, the result being that numerous *ʿatābā* verses remain incomplete. It is common to hear poets boast about their success in the game of *tatlīt*.

---

[7] *Al-Mashriq*, St. Joseph University, Beirut.

As indicated above, the *ʿatābā* verse is followed by a choral rendition of a *mījanā* hemistich. This rendition, in contrast to the poet's *nathr* rendition of the verses, invariably makes use of the *mījanā* proto-tune, perhaps with a slight variance in rhythm. It is metred, always falling into four-beat measures or divisions. Two such versions of the refrain, each repeated eighteen times, were chosen from a *ʿatābā* and *mījanā* exchange between Zaghlūl al-Dāmūr and Zayn Shʿayb.[8] As it turned out, change in poetic content had no significant effect on the thirty-six choral renditions of the two lines. As in the case of the *muʿannā* proto-tune, the results obtained showed what may be described as an iambic pattern of poetic stress.

Figure 12: *Mījanā* refrain #1

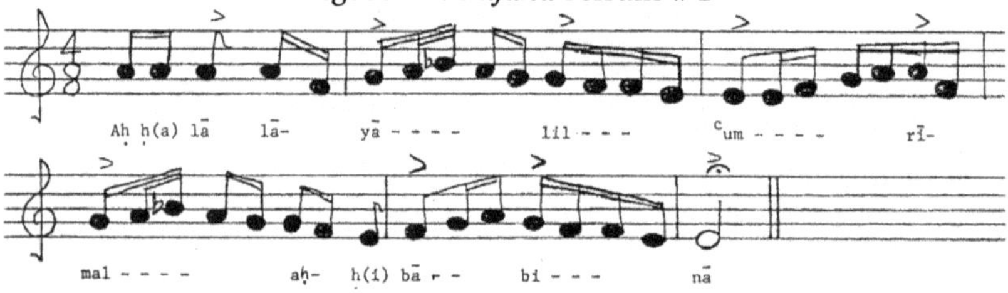

Recording 13: A recording by the author can be found at https://hdl.handle.net/20.500.12434/b4508329.[9]

Poetry *Aḥlā layāli l-ʿumri malʾa ḥbābina*
'The best nights in (our) life are when we meet with our loved ones'

---

[8] Zayn Shʿayb was a longstanding member of Zaghlūl's *jawqa* ('*zajal* group'), known for his excellent improvisational skills, especially in verbal duels.

[9] Note that the tune sung is for another *mījanā* refrain. The words are different, but the tune is the same.

Poetic scansion *Aḥ lā la yā lil ʿum ri mal ʾaḥ bā bi nā*

— — ᴗ — — — ᴗ — — — ᴗ —

Musical duration in syllables ᴗ ᴗ — ᴗ ᴗ — — — — — — — — — — — — — — — — —

Musical accent ᴗ ᴗ —́ ᴗ ᴗ —́ —́ —́ — — —́ — — — —́ —́ —́ (> > > > > > > >)

Musically speaking *lil* and *bi* have weaker accents than the syllables preceding them. Since the refrain has a four-beat measure, and since the strongest beat within any one of the measures is usually the first beat, *yā* and *bā*, receive stronger accents than *lil* and *bi*. Superimposing then the poetic line upon the musical line, the strong musical accents coincide with the following syllables:

— —́ ᴗ —́ — —́ ᴗ —́ — —́ ᴗ —́

The second *mījanā* refrain has a different pitch level but it employs the same melodic mode. It also shows a slight difference in rhythmic treatment, but the basic accents and the basic conception of the tune are the same as those of the first rendition.

Figure 13: *Mījanā* refrain #2

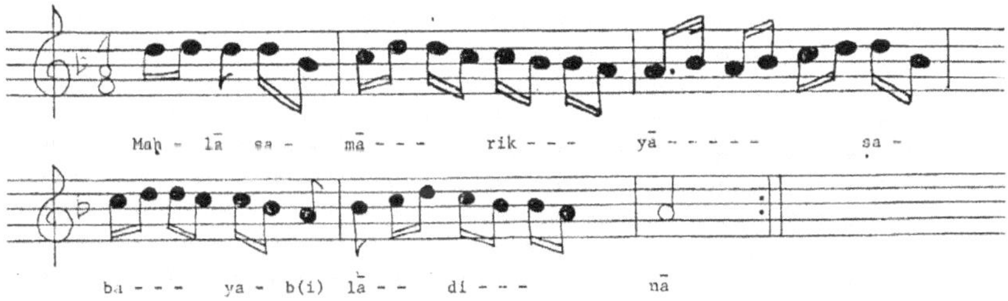

Poetry *Ma ḥlā samārik yā ṣabāya blādinā*
'How beautiful is your dark colour, O young women of our country (Lebanon)'

Poetic scansion *Maḥ lā sa mā rik yā ṣa bā ya-b lā di nā*

— — ᴗ — — — ᴗ — — — ᴗ —

Musical duration in syllables ⏑ ⏑ – ⏑ ⏑ –
Musical accent ⏑ ⏑ –̂ ⏑ ⏑ –̂ – ˇ – –̂ – – – ˇ –̂ – ˇ – –̂ – ˇ – –̂ – – –

(The sign [ˇ] indicates weaker accents in each case because of syllable position in the middle of the measure except for *ṣa* which coincides with the fourth beat.)

The strong accents produce the following stress pattern in the poetic line:

– –́ ⏑ –́ – – –́ ⏑ –́ – – –́ ⏑ –́

On the other hand, the typical *ʿatābā* verse scans as follows:

⏑ – – – / ⏑ – – – / ⏑ – –

resembling a form of the *wāfir fuṣḥā* metre called *al-maʿṣūb*. The fourth hemistich in the *bayt* is always one syllable shorter than the rest, although the last syllable is always extra-long. The following *bayt*,[10] for example, scans ⏑ – – – / ⏑ – – – / ⏑ – –o in the first hemistich.

1 *Ya ʾalbī ghiṭṭ[i] bi-d-damʿāt[i] wi-rsūm*
⏑ – – – / ⏑ – – – / ⏑ – –o
'My heart, immerse yourself in tears and draw'

2 *[L]-ḥabīb il-ʾalib aḥla khṭūṭ[i] wi-rsūm*
⏑ – – ⏑ – – – – ⏑ – –o
'For my heart's beloved the most beautiful lines and picture'

3 *[W]-idhā baddū kifālit ḥūb[i] wi-rsūm*
⏑ – – – / ⏑ – – – / ⏑ – –o
'And if she (the beloved) wants a love pledge (bail) and fees (tax money)'

---

[10] The *bayt* is by Zaghlūl al-Dāmūr in the Beit Miri verbal duel encounter of 1972.

4 *Ta ʾidfaʿ niṣṣi ʿumrī ʿa li-ḥsāb*
ᴗ _ _ _ / ᴗ _ _ / ᴗ _ _$_{o}$
'I shall pay half of my life as an advance on the account'

In the second hemistich, the apparent syllabic difference in the first two feet is caused by the poet's preference of *ʾalib* to *ʾalb[i]* (or ᴗ _ to _ ᴗ), both words being permissible dialectal readings. Read as *[L]-ḥabīb il-ʾalb[i] aḥla khṭūṭ[i] wi-rsūm*, we obtain ᴗ _ _ _ / ᴗ _ _ _ / ᴗ _ _$_{o}$. The third hemistich yields the same syllabic pattern. The fourth, which is one syllable shorter, gives ᴗ _ _ _ / ᴗ _ _ _ / ᴗ _$_{o}$, if syllables 8 and 9 are transposed in accordance with the legitimate reading, *ʿal-ḥisāb* (_ ᴗ _$_{o}$) instead of the equally legitimate *ʿa li-ḥsāb* (ᴗ _ _$_{o}$). I mention all this to emphasise that inadequate knowledge of the dialect may confuse the pattern of syllables and feet in *ʿatābā*.

Over and above dialectal considerations, the first three *ʿatābā* hemistichs may, at times, contain ten, nine, or even eight syllables rather than eleven. The loss of the first short syllable of the foot is quite frequent (ᴗ _ _ _ becomes _ _ _). A sort of *kharm* (deletion of first short syllable from the foot) takes place, to employ a term from books on traditional *fuṣḥā* where the phenomenon is limited to the beginning of lines. In the second and third feet of an *ʿatābā* hemistich, short syllables may also drop altogether, but in such cases extra-long syllables are always involved and a brief *waqfa* ('pause, stop') is used to compensate for syllabic quantity. At times, the foot ᴗ _ _ _ reverts to ᴗ _ _ ᴗ, causing a change in the succeeding foot as in the following:

ᴗ _ _ _ / ᴗ _ _ ᴗ / _ _ _

In other words, the last foot changes from ᴗ _ _ to _ _ _. The *ʿatābā bayt* that follows illustrates the loss of the first short syllable and the changes that may occur in the last two feet:

1 *Mihrī yawmi ḥash ir-rikāb biʿlāh*
_ _ _ / ᴗ _ _ ᴗ / _ _ _o
'I mount my steed in the thick of the battle'

2 *Wi-kam mihrah shtahit la-ykūn baʿlāh*
ᴗ _ _ _ / ᴗ _ _ _ p _ _o
'And how many a mare had wished that he would be her Baal (lord, husband, stallion)'

3 *Bitaʿrif ʿan Ilāh il-ʿarish bi-ʿlāh*[11]
ᴗ _ _ _ / ᴗ _ _ ᴗ / _ _ _o
'You're quite knowledgeable about God in his Heaven'

4 *Ka-ʾannak min malāyikti s-samā*
ᴗ _ _ _ / ᴗ _ _ _ / ᴗ _
'As though you were one of Heaven's angels'

In addition to the change from ᴗ _ _ _ to _ _ _ in the first foot of the first hemistich, there are two occurrences of ᴗ _ _ ᴗ instead of ᴗ _ _ _ and two changes in the basic and more common ᴗ _ _: in one case (hemistich 2) the short syllable of the foot is lost after a long syllable (*kūn*) and a short *waqfa*, and, in another case (hemistichs 1 and 3), a transposition of a long syllable for the short one takes place. These are the only variations on the most frequent ᴗ _ _ _ / ᴗ _ _ _ / ᴗ _ _, which can occur in a *bayt* of *ʿatābā*.

Framed by the *mījanā* refrain, the *ʿatābā* verse is rendered in a typical *nathr* style, where stresses, as musical accent shows,

[11] Note that *bi-ʿlāh* is a contraction of the *fuṣḥā bi-ʿulāh* ('in His heights/Heaven').

do not follow a regular pattern in the first three hemistichs. An interesting development, however, takes place towards the end of the *bayt*, and specifically in the fourth hemistich of the scores of *ʿatābā* examples studied. The last few musical notes in the fourth hemistich in each case revert to a pattern of accent that coincides with that of the ensuing *mījanā* refrain, to affect, as it were, a smooth transition from *ʿatābā* to *mījanā*. The *ʿatābā bayt* below was sung by Dr Ajami and was then followed by the typical *mījanā* refrain. The first hemistich of the *bayt* was set to two different melodic lines (lines one and two below), the second to a third musical line. In the last hemistich and its repetition, the singer anticipates the *mījanā* proto-tune (lines four and five below).

Figure 14: *ʿAtābā*

ᶜAtābā
Ta rak tā ᶜan hi - mūm mil 'al bi tim lī - - - -
I let her relate [dictate] the troubles of the heart
Ta ra ka tā - ᶜan hi - mūm mil 'alb tim lī
I let her relate [dictate] the troubles of the heart
Ta add il ᶜum ur hā bis ᶜar ri dāyb - - -
Then I would spend my life locking up [protecting] the saliva
Ḍāl ligh mi zī nī ᶜal ᶜa tim bi' shaᶜ a nā
Keep on winking [even] in the dark, I will see you
Dāl ligh mi zī- nī- ᶜal- ᶜa- tim bi i nā

Recording 14: A recording of the *ʿatābā* by the author can be found at https://hdl.handle.net/20.500.12434/edce4ce1.

The musical transcription of the pertinent *ʿatābā* hemistichs yields the following poetic scansion and the following stresses derived from musical accent:

Taraktā ʿan himūm il-ʾalib timlī
⏑ –́ – –́ ⏑ –́ – ⏑́ – – –́
or – ⏑
Taraktā ʿan himūm il-ʾalib timlī
⏑ – –́ – ⏑ –́ – ⏑ – –́ –́
Ta ʾaḍḍ il-ʿumur ḥābis ʿarriḍāb
⏑ –́ – ⏑́ – –́ – –́ ⏑ –́o
or – ⏑

Comparing the stress pattern in the last *ʿatābā* hemistich with the *mījanā* proto-tune, we discover the following coincidence:

ʿatābā ⏑ –́ – ⏑́ – –́ – –́ ⏑ –́o
or – ⏑
mījanā – –́ ⏑ –́ – – –́ ⏑ –́ – – –́ ⏑ –́

Given this result, we can conclude with certainty that a verse of *ʿatābā* commences with a free pattern of stress and ends with a pattern resembling that of *rajaz* rather than that of the *wāfir*, which, in its most prevalent form, ⏑ – ⏑ ⏑ – / ⏑ – ⏑ ⏑ – / ⏑ – –, shows either this:

⏑ – ⏑́ ⏑ –̌ / ⏑ – ⏑́ ⏑ –̌ / ⏑ –́ –̌

or this pattern of stress:

⏑ –́ ⏑ ⏑ –̌ / ⏑ –́ ⏑ ⏑ –̌ / ⏑ –́ –̌.

The *ʿatābā* metre, however, bears a close resemblance to the *maʿṣūb* variety of *wāfir* (⏑ – – – / ⏑ – – – / ⏑ – –) with, as we have seen above, possible minor modifications (usually transpositions of a short syllable with a long one or vice versa) for dialectal reasons. The music confirms this, since short poetic syllables are consistently sung to notes with shorter durations, preserving, as it were, the foot-pattern of the *maʿṣūb wāfir* metre in al-Khalīl's system. The *ʿatābā* poet's preoccupation with syllabic quantity is further illustrated in the pronunciation, during delivery, of extra-long syllables and in the frequent use of *waqfas*. Cognizant of the syllabic composition of the various feet in the metre, the poet sometimes shortens an extra-long syllable to a short one, affecting as he does, the morphology of certain words:[12]

> *Ya shakh Tawfīʾ[i] mā lī ʿizz[i] baʿdāk*
> ᴗ _ _ _ / ᴗ _ _ _ / ᴗ _ _o
> 'After you, Sheikh Tawfīq, there is no glory left for me'

In this hemistich *yā* is shortened to *ya* and *shaykh* is pronounced *shakh* in order to obtain from the combination of the two words a short and long syllable (ᴗ _), which are the first two syllables in the first *ʿatābā* foot. Similarly, knowledge of metre, and consciousness of syllabic quantity, allows the poet to render the second hemistich of the *bayt* in one of two acceptable dialectal readings. Either

> *Ghibit ʾiw ṭāl[i] ʿannī yawm[i] buʿdāk*
> ᴗ _ _ _ / ᴗ _ _ _ / ᴗ _ _o
> 'You went away and the days of separation were very long for me'

or

> *Ghib-tiw ṭāl[i] ʿannī yawm[i] buʿdāk*
> _ _ _ / ᴗ _ _ _ / ᴗ _ _o

In the first instance there is a short *waqfa* after *ghibit*, followed by the inclusion of the glottal stop *ʾi* for the sole purpose of producing a long syllable composed of the glottal stop and the ensuing silent consonant-conjunction *w*, and therefore for the purpose

---

[12] See below. *Shaykh* instead of *shakh* and the proper *baʿadak* instead of *baʿdāk* would have jarred the rhythm of the whole *bayt*.

of producing a second long syllable in the foot ⏑ _ _ _. The second reading achieves all this by forging a liaison between *ghibt* and the conjunction, at the expense, of course, of causing *kharm* which does not seem to affect the quantity of the foot. This is because *ṭāl* is pronounced longer here to compensate for the loss of the first syllable.

In his brief discussion of *ʿatābā*, Abdel-Nour[13] claims that the *ʿatābā* hemistich is reduced to the *fuṣḥā wāfir* metre, ⏑ _ ⏑ ⏑ _ / ⏑ _ ⏑ ⏑ _ / ⏑ _ _, and he adds that the foot ⏑ _ ⏑ ⏑ _ transforms into _ ⏑ _ _, as it is the case, in his words, "dans la prosodie classique" ("in classical prosody").[14] The example he gives in support of this transformation is the following:[15]

[N] khiṭīṭī rabbina byughfur khaṭākī
⏑ _ _ _ ⏑ _ _ _ ⏑ _ _
'If you sin, God will forgive your sins'

[N] ramāki d-dahr[i] bi-shāmū khaṭākī
⏑ _ _ _ ⏑ _ _ _ ⏑ _ _
'If time slings its arrows at you, it will miss'

[W]-ʿa shaṭṭ il-baḥr[i] law sirʿit khaṭākī
⏑ _ _ _ ⏑ _ _ _ ⏑ _ _
'If your steps speed across the seashore'

Nabat fī ramlit il-māliḥ ʿishāb
⏑ _ _ _ ⏑ _ _ _ ⏑ _o
'Green grass will sprout upon the salted sands'

The assertion that ⏑ _ _ _, the basic foot of *wāfir*, may change into _ ⏑ _ _, the basic foot of *ramal*, goes against the rules of

[13] Abdel-Nour 1957, 103–4.

[14] Abdel-Nour 1957, 104.

[15] Abdel-Nour 1957, 104.

Arabic metrics. The books on *ʿarūḍ* never mention such a transformation. In addition, the *bayt* of *ʿatābā* that he offers as example does not support his assertion. The only possible explanation is that Abdel-Nour scanned the *bayt* by reading the unvowelled consonants at the beginning of the first three hemistichs as *in*, *in* and *iw* respectively, giving each hemistich an extra-long syllable:

– ⏑ – – / – ⏑ – – / – ⏑ – –
– ⏑ – – / – ⏑ – – / – ⏑ – –
– ⏑ – – / – ⏑ – – / – ⏑ – –

The resulting pattern then becomes that of the *fuṣḥā ramal* metre. The problem here is that Abdel-Nour is imposing a *fuṣḥā* reading, *in khiṭīṭī*, *in ramākī* and *iw ʿa shaṭṭ* in order to satisfy the demand that no line in *fuṣḥā* may begin with an unvowelled consonant.

The situation is not the same in Arabic dialect. Phonetically speaking, the first syllables and *ʿa* is where the scansion of the hemistichs should begin. Deleting, therefore, the first forced long syllables, we obtain:

⏑ – – – / ⏑ – – – / ⏑ – –
⏑ – – – / ⏑ – – – / ⏑ – –
⏑ – – – / ⏑ – – – / ⏑ – –

which with reference to the fourth hemistich,

Nabat fī ramlit il-māliḥ ʿishāb
⏑ – – – / ⏑ – – – / ⏑ –o

yields the form of *wāfir* that characterises *ʿatābā*. Even if the poet were to read the hemistichs as Abdel-Nour would have them read (and this is not unusual in particular metres and particular situations), the metre would still be that of the *wāfir* as long as the stress pattern of the *wāfir* is used as the point of reference.

***

Al-qaṣīd. Of the major critics on Lebanese *zajal* only Lecerf and Tawfīq ʿAwwād identify the *qaṣīd* as a full-fledged genre. Lecerf lists it under "Les Genres Dits" ('Spoken Genres') as opposed to "Les Genres Chantés," ('Sung Genres') although it is well-known that the *qaṣīd* can be both sung and declaimed. He defines the *qaṣīd* as a long piece with a common rhyme for all the first hemistichs and another for all the second ones. Tawfīq ʿAwwād, who uses *maʿannā* and *zajal* interchangeably, divides *maʿannā* or *zajal* into *maṭlaʿ qaṣīd* (lit. 'proem of a *qaṣīd*') and *qarrādī*, thus erasing the distinction that exists between the metrical characteristics of *qarrādī* and *qaṣīd*.

Abdel-Nour does not seem to be aware of *qaṣīd* altogether, and both Whaybeh and Nakhleh treat it as a kind of *maʿannā*. Nakhleh, however, recognises three metres in which *qaṣīd* as a subtype of *maʿannā* may appear. The first, according to him, is none other than the *wāfir* of al-Khalīl's metrics and the other two have respectively the same metres of *al-maʿannā al-maṭlaʿ* and *al-maʿannā al-badālī*, whose metres he does not spell out. Whaybeh is even less clear. He lists, for example, under *maʿannā* twelve *anwāʿ* ('kinds, types'), five of which are *qaṣīds* which differ in rhyme and verse structure. Curiously, two of these *qaṣīds* are given the same name, *al-maʿannā al-qaṣīd*,[16] although one scans according to the *yaʿqūbi* metre of Whaybeh's metrical classification, and the other in the Khalīlian *sarīʿ* metre.

The poets of *zajal* themselves recognise *qaṣīd* as a separate genre with specific functions and clear formal characteristics

[16] See Whaybeh 1952, 64–72.

which differentiate it from *maʿannā* when that term is used as both a genre and a metre of vernacular poetry. In an interview conducted for this study with Lebanon's most popular *zajal* poet, Joseph al-Hāshim, known to his admirers by his pen name Zaghlūl al-Dāmūr ('the humming dove of Dāmūr'), Zaghlūl asserted that *qaṣīd* is a separate genre which exists in three distinctive metres. He identified these metres as 'the long one', or the 'metre of *maʿannā*', 'the middle one', and 'the short one' or the *badālī qaṣīd*, as he termed it. He then proceeded to give an example of each. When he was pressed to identify them more clearly, he responded by giving further examples of each.

What is significant about Zaghlūl's naïve attempt to define the metres of the *qaṣīd* is his appeal to length: long, middle and short. In other words, syllable quantity as well as syllable number seem to be, at least in the minds of the poets of *zajal*, the main guideline for the composition of *qaṣīds* as well as a measuring rod that distinguishes one *qaṣīd* from another. Nowhere in the interview does Zaghlūl speak of the role of stress, but this does not necessarily mean that stress does not play a significant role. Al-Khalīl himself did not specifically speak of stress (*nabr*) but his system, as has been shown, does indeed take stress into consideration.

At any rate, the scansion of Zaghlūl's examples and other *qaṣīds* from popular verbal duels have demonstrated without any doubt that the metres of the *qaṣīd* corresponded to three of al-Khalīl's metres, the *rajaz*, the *wāfir* and the *sarīʿ*, respectively. In addition to scansion, another proof came from attempting to sing the three *qaṣīds* to tunes associated with genres of comparable metres. First, the long *qaṣīd* was sung to the tune of the *maʿannā* refrain. That proved to be quite easy, indicating that the *rajaz* metre, the metre employed in *maʿannā* is also the metre of the long *qaṣīd*. Second, the middle *qaṣīd* was sung as a *ʿatābā bayt*, and again the tune accommodated the metre, giving rise to the possibility that *wāfir* is the metre of the middle *qaṣīd*. On the other hand, singing the short *qaṣīd* to the tunes of *maʿannā* and *ʿatābā* proved impossible with *maʿannā* and significantly jarred the rhythm of *ʿatābā*. The short *qaṣīd*, as we shall see below, scans in the *sarīʿ* metre which has particular rhythmic characteristics.

One important formal feature which has escaped the attention of all writers on *zajal* is the use in *qaṣīd* of *taṣrīʿ* ('giving the same rhyme to the first two hemistichs of the poem') as was the case with the *fuṣḥā qaṣīda*. In the pre-Islamic *qaṣīda*, *taṣrīʿ* was used at the beginning of the formal *fuṣḥā* poem and, at times, within the poem as a device signalling a new theme or a variation on an old one. This seems to be precisely the case in the Lebanese *qaṣīd*, which gives evidence of its relation to the *fuṣḥā* prototype, at least at this formal level. More importantly, the word *qaṣīd* and the word *qaṣīda* derive from *qaṣada* which means at once 'to intend' and 'to sing', both significations characterizing the *fuṣḥā* and vernacular poem. *Qaṣīd* in *zajal* is always an occasional poem with a specific purpose (*qaṣd*). In most cases it resembles the major genres of *fuṣḥā* poetry: *madīḥ* ('panegyric verse'), *hijāʾ* ('satire'), *fakhr* ('boasting'), and *rithāʾ* ('elegy'). It is always at least four verses long and may reach fifty or more.

The typical *qaṣīd* has the following rhyme scheme:

___a ___a
___b ___a

___b ___a
___b ___a
___b ___c
___a

In other words, after *taṣrīʿ* in the first line, the *qaṣīd* adopts two rhymes, one for all the first hemistichs and one for the second ones. In the vast majority of cases, a closure is signalled by introducing a new rhyme in the last *bayt*. A final hemistich employing the rhyme of the first *bayt* is then added as a *rujūʿ* ('return') to that rhyme.

In a long *qaṣīd* the rhyme scheme may break as

___a ___a
___b ___a
___b ___a
___b ___a
___b ___a
___c ___c
___d ___c
___d ___c
___d ___c
___e ___e
___f ___e
___f ___e
___f ___g
___e

or

___a ___a
___b ___a
___c ___c
___d ___c
___e ___e
___f ___e
etc.

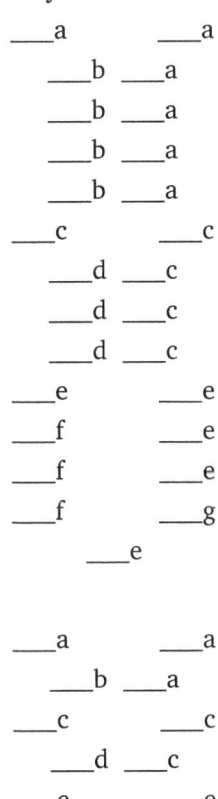

This time around it is without a *rujūʿ*. When such form is employed, the last syllable in the last line is lengthened perceptibly to indicate closure. In rare cases, mostly written as opposed to orally declaimed *qaṣīds*, the rhyme scheme is exactly that of a typical *fuṣḥā qaṣīda*:

___a ___a
___b ___a
___c ___a
___d ___a
___e ___a
etc.

Notwithstanding such rare examples, it seems to me that *qaṣīd*'s strict rhyme patterns play an important role in differentiating it from other *nathr* genres. No *maʿannā*, for example, will end with a final hemistich as the *qaṣīd* does, though the use of *taṣrīʿ* and separate rhymes for first and second hemistichs are the general rule in *maʿannā* also.

Figure 15: The short *qaṣīd*

Recording 15: A recording by the author can be found at https://hdl.handle.net/20.500.12434/53b3aa1a.

Figure 16: The middle *qaṣīd*

Recording 16: A recording by the author can be found at https://hdl.handle.net/20.500.12434/0bb108db.

Figure 17: The long *qaṣīd*

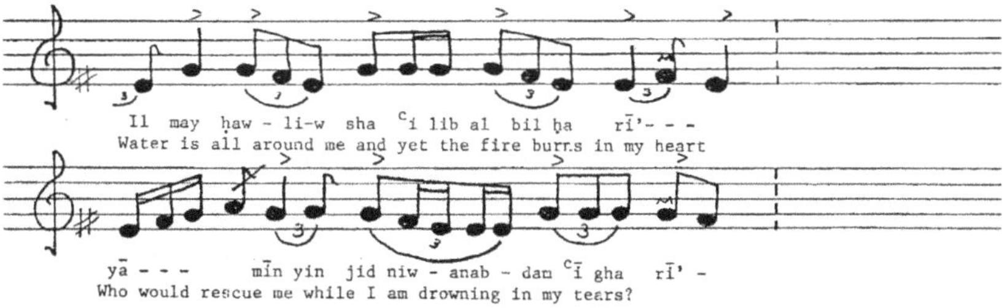

Recording 17: A recording by the author can be found at https://hdl.handle.net/20.500.12434/2f2f70df.

In its three metres, the *qaṣīd* belongs to the *nathr* style. Its stress pattern, therefore, is irregular. Because, unlike *maʿannā*, *ʿatābā* and *mījanā*, the *qaṣīd* is declaimed or sung without an accompanying choral refrain, it is difficult to ascertain whether its metres follow the stress patterns of the *fuṣḥā*'s *rajaz*, *wāfir* and *sarīʿ* metres which traditional scansion usually yields. The music, however, makes clear that musical durations correspond in most cases to poetic syllable durations, thus obviating the role of the chorus which brings about this regularity in *maʿannā*, for example. The musical transcriptions thereby offer a guide to the probable *fuṣḥā* metrical prototype, at least in terms of syllable quantity. For the purpose of illustrating this correspondence between musical duration and poetic syllable quantity, the eighth notes (ε) are considered long notes while the sixteenth notes (ξ) are short. In those cases where the single beat is divided into three eighth notes as a triplet figure (♪♪♪) instead of a duple (♫), we have counted them as long syllable durations, although they are slightly shorter than the usual eighth notes. Thus the following picture emerges for the three *qaṣīds*:

The short *qaṣīd*

	L'in sān law mā ki lim tub tin 'āl
poetic scansion	_ _[⏑] _ _ _ ⏑ _ _ _[17]
	⏑ _
musical scansion	_ _ _ _ ⏑ ⏑ ⏑ ⏑ _
	Kān Al lāh byikh la 'ū tim thāl
poetic scansion	_[⏑] _ _ _ ⏑ _ _ _
musical scansion	_ _ _ _ _ _ _ _

The middle *qaṣīd*

	ʿA lay nā 'add(i) mal 'iy yām(i) jā rū
poetic scansion	⏑ _ _ _[⏑] _ _ _[⏑] _ _[18]
musical scansion	⏑ _ _ _ _ _ _ _ _
	Ma fī hun ba ḥir nay ghū ṣub ghi mā rū
poetic scansion	⏑ _ _ _ ⏑ _ _ _ ⏑ _ _[19]
	⏑ _
musical scansion	⏑ ⏑⏑ _ ⏑ _ ⏑ _ ⏑ ⏑ _ _
	_

[17] *ki lim* = ⏑ _ or *kil mi* = _ ⏑ are both possible when read.

[18] Note that the short syllable (⏑) is inserted as a possible reading of the hemistich.

[19] Note that *ba ḥir* (⏑ _) may be read as *baḥ ri* (_ ⏑).

The long *qaṣīd*

	Il mayy haw līw sha ʿi lib ʾal bil ḥa rīʾ
poetic scansion	_ _[ᴗ] _ _ _ ᴗ _ _ _ ᴗ _
musical scansion	_ _ _ _ _ ᴗ ᴗ _ _ _ _
	Yā mīn yin jid ni-w a-nab dam ʿī gha rīʾ
poetic scansion	_ _[ᴗ]_ _ _ ᴗ _ _ _ ᴗ _
musical scansion	ᴗᴗᴗ _ _ _ ᴗᴗ ᴗ _ _ _ _ _
	_

Since triplet eighth notes have a somewhat ambiguous quality, being neither fully long nor fully short in duration, they provide the reciter with the freedom to improvise without having to be locked in a strict conformance to musical and poetic duration. The apparent discrepancies above are only found in those notes of equivocal duration. In some cases (e.g., musical syllable six in middle *qaṣīd* hemistich 2 and the two penultimate syllables in the two hemistichs of the long *qaṣīd*) the long musical syllables are the last syllables in their respective triplet figures and are therefore weaker than the preceding ones. In general, there is a tendency for these durational discrepancies to exist toward the end of hemistichs, which may be explained by the desire on the part of the reciter or singer to make a contrast with his final long syllable.

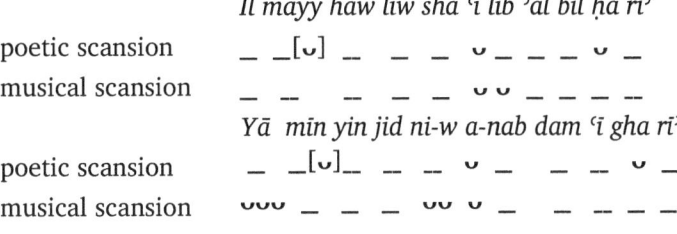

The proof that we are dealing with the three *fuṣḥā* metres *sarīʿ*, *wāfir* and *rajaz* comes, of course, from scanning a large number of sung and declaimed *qaṣīds* where in almost every case the patterns of feet associated with these metres is evident. With the exception of the frequent appearance of _ ᴗ _ instead of _ _ ᴗ _ in the first feet of the short and the long *qaṣīds* and _ _ _ instead of ᴗ _ _ _ in the first foot of the middle *qaṣīd*, and the occasional transposition of short and long syllables where variant dialectal readings are acceptable (e.g., *kilimtū* 'his word' ᴗ _ _, as opposed to *kilmitū* _ ᴗ _, in the first hemistich of the short *qaṣīd* cited above) the patterns _ _ ᴗ _ / _ _ ᴗ _ / _ _, ᴗ _ _ _ / ᴗ _ _ _ / ᴗ _ _ and _ _ ᴗ _ / _ _ ᴗ _ / _ _ ᴗ _ emerged. These are standard configurations of the *sarīʿ*, *wāfir* and *rajaz fuṣḥā* metres, respectively.

Even in early written versions of *qaṣīds*, these same metres emerge despite the frequent use of desinential inflections. In all the *qaṣīd* samples studied, there is a greater metrical stability than that obtained from *maʿannā, ʿatābā* and *mījanā,* for example. In the writings of sixteenth-century Maronite clerics, the metres are generally managed with utmost care, though often at the expense of proper morphology and syntax. One such middle *qaṣīd,* dated 1517, is contained in No. 265 in Assemanus' *Codices Arabici.* It is by one Elia Abrahamī, "discipulo domini Petri Patriarchae Maronitarum" ('student of Lord Peter, the Patriach of the Maronites'). The following reading of Abrahamī's middle *qaṣīd* takes into account acceptable vernacular pronunciation of particular *fuṣḥā* words and is guided by the popular musical tune associated with middle *qaṣīds* in modern *zajal*:

(a) *Wajadtu d-dahra dūlābin yadūrī*
ᴗ _ _ _ / ᴗ _ _ _ / ᴗ _ _
'I have found life (time) to be a wheel that turns'

(b) *Wa-lā faraḥan yadūmu wa-lā surūrī*
ᴗ _ ᴗ ᴗ _ / ᴗ _ ᴗ ᴗ _ / ᴗ _ _
'And neither happiness nor joy lasts'

Or:

(b') *Wa-lā farḥan yadūmu w-lā surūrī*
ᴗ _ _ _ / ᴗ _ _ _ / ᴗ _ _

(c) *Wajadtu n-nāsa kullahumū sakārā*

⏑ _ _ _ / ⏑ _ ⏑ ⏑ _ / ⏑ _ _

or *kulluhmū*

_ _ _

'I have found all people to be drunkards'

(d) *Wa-kaʾsa l-mawti baynahumū yadūrī*

⏑ _ _ _ / ⏑ _ ⏑ ⏑ _ / ⏑ _ _

or *baynahmū*

_ _ _

'And the cup of death passes from one to another'

(e) *Mulūkun ʾabnū quṣūran thumma ʿizzan*

⏑ _ _ _ [_] / ⏑ _ _ _ / ⏑ _ _

'Kings built palaces, then glory'

(f) *Wa-lā dāmū l-mulūku wa-lā l-quṣūrī*

⏑ _ _ _ / ⏑ _ ⏑ ⏑ _ / ⏑ _ _

'But neither the kings nor the palaces lasted'

(g) *Wa-ṭūla ʿumrī ʾadūr bayn il-maʾābir*

⏑ _ ⏑ _ _ / ⏑ _$_o$ _ _ / ⏑ _ _

'And all my life I have walked among tombs'

(h) *Wa-lā ʾadrī ʾayna qābrī*[20] *fī l-qubūrī*

⏑ _ _ _ [_] / ⏑ _ _ _ / ⏑ _ _

'Not knowing which one among them is my tomb'

(h') *W-la ʾadrī ʾayna qabrī fī l-qubūrī*

⏑ _ _ _ / ⏑ _ _ _ / ⏑ _ _

It is quite apparent from the above that a partial *fuṣḥā* reading of hemistichs a, b, c, d, and f yields a *wāfir* scansion with the occasional substitution of the acceptable ⏑ _ ⏑ ⏑ _ (*mufāʿalatun*) for

[20] Note the possible extra-long syllable (_$_o$).

⏑ _ _ _ (*mafāʿīlun*). This is so despite the obvious grammatical mistakes in hemistich a (*dulābun* or *dulābin* for *dulāban*) and in hemistich f (*dāmū* for *dāma*), and the liberties taken to preserve the rhyme letter *ri* in the rhyme scheme

___a ___a
___b ___a
___c ___a
___d ___a

Three exceptions are hemistichs e, g, and h, where a strict *fuṣḥā* reading all but destroys the scansion. However, if *mulūkun* in e is read *muluk*, *ṭūla* in g is read *ṭūl*, and *wa lā adrī* in h is rendered as *w-la-adrī* as in h, all the feet will then become ⏑ _ _ _. It follows that in order to achieve proper readings of early *zajals*, one should first gain a sense of the tune associated with each genre, then one should decide, in light of the music, which words should be read as *fuṣḥā* words, with or without inflexion, and which words, though written in the resemblance of *fuṣḥā* or the vernacular (e.g., *abnū* 'built' for *banaw*) should be retained to preserve the intended metre.

***

Al-ḥidā. In his brief comments on *ḥidā*,[21] Abdel-Nour decries the fact that the annals of history record only rare examples of this genre which he assumes has gone out of fashion. He gives two short examples of *ḥidā* and claims that the genre employs the *basīṭ* metre, a variety of *qarrādī* and rarely the *rajaz*, all this without supplying proof. This is quite curious, especially since *ḥidā* enjoys great popularity in the works of all the modern poets I have

[21] Abdel-Nour 1957, 24–25.

encountered, and since its tune is quite familiar to all aficionados of *zajal*. Moreover, the genre is an integral part of the highly structured verbal duel where the duellers shift from *maʿannā* and *qarrādī* to *ḥidā* and *shurūqī* in order to add variety.

Abdel-Nour's first example was supposedly given to him by the poet William Ṣaʿb, who got it from Sheikh Nāyef Talḥūq from the town of ʿAytāt in the Shūf district of Lebanon. According to Abdel-Nour's sources, the verses were composed in 1750 during a military parade in Shwayfāt in the presence of the ruling Emir.[22] This may very well be the case, but Abdel-Nour has unfortunately written out the verses without any reference to the tune to which they were sung, thus misrepresenting their actual syllabic quantity. After such misrepresentation, scansion becomes a bewildering task. To illustrate, I shall first scan the first two verses as they are written by Abdel-Nour, then write them and scan them again, this time according to the popular tune of *ḥidā*:

Yā mīrinā jīnāk i ghārā	*Bi zlām i wi khyūlan ta ʿinnā*
– – ᴗ – – – ᴗ – –	– – ᴗ – – – ᴗ – –
'O Emir! We've come to you charging forth'	'With men and experienced horses'
Ḥinnā siyājan li-l-ʿadhārā	*Ḥūṣun ʿala z-zināt i ḥinnā*
– – ᴗ – – – ᴗ – –	– – ᴗ – ᴗ – ᴗ – –
'We are a fence that protects the virgins (beautiful women)'	'and a fortress; we are henna for the beautiful women'

According to the alternation of long and short syllables, the first foot seems to be – – ᴗ –, the first foot of either *rajaz* or *basīṭ*, and

[22] Abdel-Nour 1957, 25.

the rest of the syllables are either one too many for the short *rajaz* hemistich, or one or two too few for a form of *basīṭ*, as the books on *ʿarūḍ* indicate. This explains, I think, why Abdel-Nour chose not to scan the lines himself and instead gave an arbitrary designation of the metre.

With the *ḥidā* tune as a guiding principle, the lines ought to be written as follows:

Yā mīrinā jīnak ghārā	*Bi-zlā[m] wi-khyūlan taʿinnā*
_ _ ◡ _ _ _ _ _	_ _o ◡ _ _ ◡ _ _
Ḥinnā syājan li-l-ʿadhārā	*Ḥūsūn[i] ʿla z-zīnat ḥinnā*
_ _ _ _ _ ◡ _ _	_ _ _ _ _ _ _ _

Here eight syllables instead of nine obtain in each case after several long syllables have been shortened and several short ones have been assimilated with long ones in accordance with the tune of *ḥidā*. In our discussion of *maʿannā* above, we have seen how _ _ ◡ _ sometimes reverts to _ ◡ _ _ or _ _ _ _. With this observation in mind, we can assume with certainty that we are dealing with a form resembling the short form of *rajaz*: _ _ ◡ _, _ _ ◡ _, with the short syllable often becoming a long one.

The second example that Abdel-Nour offers bears little resemblance to the orally improvised pieces of *ḥidā* in the works of the modern poets. His example is taken from Rashīd Nakhleh's *Dīwān* which is famous for the author's experimentation in the metrical forms of *zajal*. Although this particular composition by Nakhleh celebrates, like most *ḥidā*, the exploits of heroes, it is not recognised by the poets I interviewed as a *ḥidā* composition.[23]

[23] For example, Zaghlūl al-Dāmūr, in an interview in Beirut in 2001.

None of them was able to sing it to the *ḥidā* tune that he associates with the genre. Also quite wrongly, I think, Abdel-Nour insists that the metre in this case consists of nine syllables divided into three equal feet, while, in reality, when the lines are declaimed, there are ten long syllables to the hemistich, divided most probably into four, three and three long syllables as follows:

Yā Yūsif beyk	*shiʾ il-khayl*	*bi-ḥṣānak*
— —— —o	— — —o	— — —
‘O Yūsif Bey,	scatter the steeds	with your horse’
Ihden bitghūṣ	*baḥr ed-dam*	*ʿāshānak*
— — ——o	— — —	— — —
‘Ihden plunges in	the sea of blood	for your sake’
ʿAynak la-tshūf	*kif hayjāt*	*fityānak*
— — — —o	— ——o	—— —
‘If your eyes saw	the courage	of your heroes’
Yā beyki ṭlūb	*shū bitrīd*	*wi-tmannā*
— —— —o	— ——o	— — —
‘O Bey, ask for	what you want	and desire!’

The absence of short syllables accounts for Abdel-Nour’s assertion that the metre in this stanza is “un autre derivé du *qarrādī*” (“another derivative of *qarrādī*”), which he considers a quantitative metre resembling *khabab* in its formal characteristics.[24] I have already shown that reference to syllable quantity alone does not lead to proper metrical description and that consideration of stress is indispensable for distinguishing the rhythmic compo-

[24] *Khabab* is a classical meter added to al-Khalīl’s metrics by al-Akhfash (d. 793). It scans as follows: _ _ / _ _ / _ _ / _ _ with a number of variations in every foot.

nents of verse. Here it is useful to add that the ten-syllable lines above will not, when sung, fit the *qarrādī* trochaic measure, nor will they accommodate the shorter *ḥidā* tune that poets associate with the metre of *ḥidā*. As will be shown below, the two short syllables in the modern pieces studied are essential to the rendition of the musical tunes.

Certainly, the term *ḥidā* itself highlights the importance of music for the proper description of the metre. In Classical Arabic *ḥidāʾ* or *ḥudāʾ* refers to the chanting of the camel caravan leader. The verb *ḥadā* (imperfect *yaḥdū*) means 'to urge (the camels) by singing'.[25] In its Lebanese context, *al-ḥidā* is a song that celebrates the valour of a leader of high repute or occasionally the death of such a person, detailing his social and moral qualities.[26] It is a *naẓm* piece with a verifiable tune, composed of several strophes, each with the following rhyme scheme:

___a ___a
___b ___b
___b ___a

or,

___a ___a
___b ___a

or (especially in older examples of the genre),

___a ___b
___a ___b
___a ___b

etc.

[25] See root *ḥ-d-w* in Lane 1984, I:532–33.

[26] Lane 1984, I:532–33.

In order to verify both the tune and the musical metre of *ḥidāʾ*, I have used field tapes recorded at different times by two different singers.[27] The transcriptions were laid out by musical phrases in a comparative scheme for the purpose of studying at once the renditions of both singers. It is shown that both adhered to the same overall musical metric structure, although there were slight differences in the duration of notes. In each hemistich the accented musical notes coincide with the poetic metrical stress pattern usually associated with the short form of *rajaz*. The modal structure of the tune comprises a minor pentachord based on the finalis d (i.e., d e f g a), each phrase beginning on the upper tone and ending on the third degree.

The syncopated stress of the second beat of the 10/8 pattern is consistent in both performances, and it is this aspect that is crucial to our determination of metrical stress, and from which we justify the musical accent pattern.

Figure 18: Superimposition
of musical rhythm and accents with poetic meter, illustrating the alignment between rhythmic beats and metrical stresses

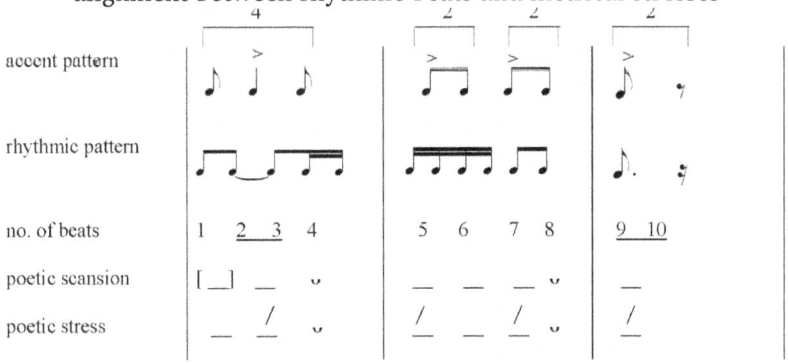

[27] The reference is to Zaghlūl al-Dāmūr and Mansour Ajami.

Although the poetic scansion does not match perfectly in terms of longs and shorts with the musical metre, the short poetic syllables are always sung to short musical syllables. In a textual hemistich, in other words, it is the third and seventh syllables that maintain the short quantity designation of the poetic metre.

The metronomical indications were obtained with the aid of a stopwatch and the stemless notes preceding the initial clefs indicate the actual beginning pitches of the respective performances:

Text #1

[R]jāli l-miruwwi rjālinā
'The men of courage are our men'

[B]yilṭā sh-sharaf bi-khyālinā
'Honour takes refuge in our shadow'

Ṭāʿit li-aydīna s-siyūf
'Swords are obedient to our hands'

[W]-ʿā ṣawtina tkirr il-ʾilūf
'Thousands (of men) answer to our voice (call)'

[W]-lamma s-siyūf tiʾḥam siyūf
'And when swords vie with swords'

[B]yirdī l-ʿidā khayyālinā
'Our horsemen vanquish the enemy'

Text #2

Law nimt[i] aw jismī wiʿī
'Whether I sleep or wake up'

Ṣibḥ iw-masa tayfik maʿī
'Your ghost is with me day and night'

Min baʿd[i] hal hajri ṭ-ṭawīl
'After this long estrangement'

Ḥallik yā Laylā tirjaʿī
'It is time you came back, Layla'

The musical transcription that follows depicts a verse (two hemistichs) at a time. Text #1 corresponds to the A lines and text #2 to the B lines. The transcription is followed by the clapping pattern derived from the chorus in each case.

Figure 19: *Ḥidā*

Recording 18: A recording by the author can be accessed at https://hdl.handle.net/20.500.12434/56dc3134.

***

Al-nadb. A genre of great popularity is *nadb* (*maṣdar*, or verbal noun, of *nadaba*)[28] which has seen rich melodic developments. It is a *naẓm* piece with a basic tune, sung at funerals, recalling the virtues of the deceased and exhorting his or her family and friends to shed tears and bewail their loss. Often the names of long-departed friends are mentioned to remind some of those present of the loss of their own dear ones. Usually, a poet of *zajal* is hired for the occasion, especially if the dead person is young or a well-known community leader. A picture of the deceased is hoisted up by one of the mourners, who walks slowly inside or around the house, followed by the poet and the friends of the deceased. The poet then starts his *nadb*, and the mourners act as a chorus repeating particular refrains at the end of stanzas. In general, the occasion is characterised by morbid seriousness; but if the deceased is a young boy or girl, the melody changes and the impression is given that the occasion is a happy one. Tambourines, drums and handclapping contribute an air of celebration characteristic of weddings rather than funerals.

The following two notations of the same *nadb* tune were transcribed separately by Professors Katz and al-Faruqi. In both, we have a simple trichord in a simple triple metre pattern. In the first notation, the musical accent is on the first and second beat of each measure, or on the first and third poetic syllable. In the second, each hemistich corresponds to a six-beat musical phrase,

---

[28] *Nadaba*: 'He wailed for, wept for, or deplored the loss of the dead man, and enumerated his good qualities and actions'. See Lane 1984, II:2779.

and strong stresses correspond with beats two and five. There are lesser stresses on one and four.

Figure 20: *Nadb*

Recording 19: A recording by the author can be accessed at https://hdl.handle.net/20.500.12434/8e1e009d.

In this piece, as in all other *nadb*s studied, the poetic scansion reveals the following arrangement of syllables: _ ᴗ _ _ _ ᴗ _ _, or a combination of two _ ᴗ _ _, if reference is made to possible division into feet. The second syllable of each foot is almost always short and, in those rare occasions where it is long, it is rendered as short when sung to the tune. The poetic stresses derived from musical accent have the following pattern: _́ ᴗ _́ _ / _́ ᴗ _́ _. It is a trochaic pattern which has been shown to characterise a short form of the *ramal fuṣḥā* metre. Only occasionally does _ ᴗ _ _ revert to ᴗ ᴗ _ _, but then the first short syllable gets the stress. This attests to the *naẓm* quality of the tune, giving syllable position in the measure more importance than syllable quantity. The following notations of three *nadb* pieces, with various measures, conform to the general tune and yield the same poetic stress—musical accent pattern as the first piece. They are introduced here in order to give an idea of the melodic possibilities of the genre:

Figure 21: *Nadb* #1

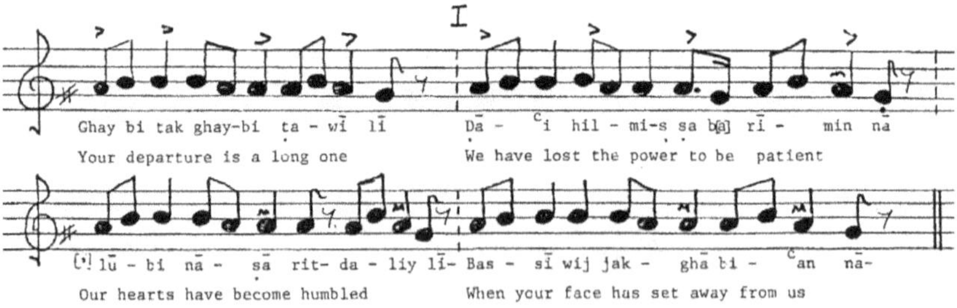

Recording 20: A recording by the author can be accessed at https://hdl.handle.net/20.500.12434/e501be1a.

Figure 22: *Nadb #2*

Recording 21: A recording by the author can be found at https://hdl.handle.net/20.500.12434/011231ce.

Figure 23: *Nadb #3*

Recording 22: A recording of this *nadb* by the author can be found at https://hdl.handle.net/20.500.12434/7b8abb9b.

Finally, two possible rhyme schemes obtain in *nadb*, either

___a ___a
___b ___a

or ___a ___b
___a ___b

The number of hemistichs varies from four to ten, with hardly any piece going beyond ten.

***

Al-ḥawraba. Ḥawraba is the term applied to a genre of *zajal* associated with *nadb*, although its metre is quite different from the short *ramal* of *nadb*. Among others, Whaybeh lists *ḥawraba* under *nadb* and implies without offering examples that both genres are metrically the same.[29] One thing is quite clear. Like *nadb*, *ḥawraba* is sung at funerals and, like *nadb*, its purpose is to elicit memories of the deceased person in the mourners. Its poetic metre and its musical tune, however, are different from those of *nadb*. They are rather those of *ḥidā*, with hardly any change in melody:

Figure 24: *Ḥawraba*

Recording 23: A recording by the author can be listened to at https://hdl.handle.net/20.500.12434/c6a4fb43.

Matching the poetic syllables with the accented musical notes, we obtain the stress pattern we have seen related to *rajaz*: _ _́ ᴗ _́ / _ _́ ᴗ _́. All this proves that *ḥawraba* is indeed a *ḥidā*, which employs the elegiac themes of *nadb*. Whaybeh's theme-oriented discussion cannot hope to address the metrical and musical complexities of this and other *zajal* genres.

Also associated with *nadb* is *nawḥ* ('wailing or lamentation for the dead') which treats themes typical of *nadb* and *ḥawraba*, but whose metre is different from both. This time around, the scansion reveals a typical *basīṭ fuṣḥā* metre with hardly any licences:

---

[29] Whaybeh 1952, 76–78.

Riḥnā ila l-qabr[i] nibki w-nirtiji l-ḥirrās

_ _́ ᴗ _́ / _́ ᴗ _́ / _ _́ ᴗ _́ / _ _́o

'We went to the tomb crying and begging the guards'

[W]-in ʾūli bi-l-lāh ʿalaykum ṭāshi minna r-rās

_ _́ ᴗ _́ / _́o ᴗ _́ / _ _́ ᴗ _́ / _ _́o

'Saying, "For God's sake, our heads are dizzy.'

Maḥbūbinā ʿindikum riddūh linā yā nās

_ _́ ᴗ _́ / _́ ᴗ _́ / _ _́o ᴗ _́ / _ _́o

'"Our beloved is with you. Give him back, O people."'

ʾĀlū ʾamalkum ʾataʿ yā ḥirʾi til-ʾanfās

_ _́ ᴗ _́ / _́ ᴗ _́ / _ _́ ᴗ _́ / _ _́o

'They said, "Your hope is gone, what a great pity."'

Unlike *nadb*, which is sung by both men and women, *nawḥ* is sung by women only, in a manner reminiscent of that of the faithful women at Christ's tomb. We recorded three renditions of the piece above in order to locate the stress pattern in every line. The result in each case revealed a uniform scheme, although in one rendition the second stress in each line proved weaker than the rest. This was so, it seems to me, because of the presence of a stressed syllable immediately following this second stressed one. The stresses break down as follows:

_ _́ ᴗ _́ / _́ ᴗ _́ / _ _́ ᴗ _́ / _ _́o
_ _́ ᴗ _́ / _́o ᴗ _́ / _ _́ ᴗ _́ / _ _́o
_ _́ ᴗ _́ / _́ ᴗ _́ / _ _́o ᴗ _́ / _ _́o
_ _́ ᴗ _́ / _́ ᴗ _́ / _ _́ ᴗ _́ / _ _́o

***

Al-zalghaṭa. In the Lebanese mountains weddings are celebrated according to ancient rituals which have been preserved intact until today. Unfortunately, city weddings have largely become westernised, doing away with most, if not all, of the traditional ceremonies that are dear to the Lebanese village and mountain folk. Village weddings are public rather than private occasions. Everyone participates in one capacity or another, some by preparing the bride and the groom for the wedding ceremony, others by welcoming them in song, dance, and music. Several women stand before the bride and the groom, and sing *zalāghīṭ* (plural of *zalghaṭa*), recounting the virtues of the newly married couple and wishing them happiness and success. After every *zalghaṭa* verse, which normally consists of four hemistichs and is called a *zalghūṭa* (n. sing.), the guests clap, both in order to express their appreciation for the message contained in the *zalghūṭa* and to signal the beginning of another verse by the same or another woman. Each one of the hemistichs starts with *Āyhā*, a meaningless two-syllable vocable whose main function is to draw attention to the hemistich that follows. After the fourth hemistich is delivered, the whole verse is ended with the recitation of a series of *lī* syllables produced by trilling the tongue at high speed in the manner of songbirds while rounding the hand over the upper lip in order to direct the sound at the bride and the groom. Besides giving a closural effect, this series of *līs* signals the guests themselves to participate and they then render individually or in unison their versions of the *lī lī lī* series. In most cases the four hemistichs have the same end-rhyme, but the tradition preserves as well a significant number of *zalāghīṭ* which rhyme a a, b a.

In the dichotomy of Arabic music, the *zalghaṭa*, as the musical transcription clearly shows, belongs to *nathr al-naghamāt*.

Figure 25: *Zalghaṭa*

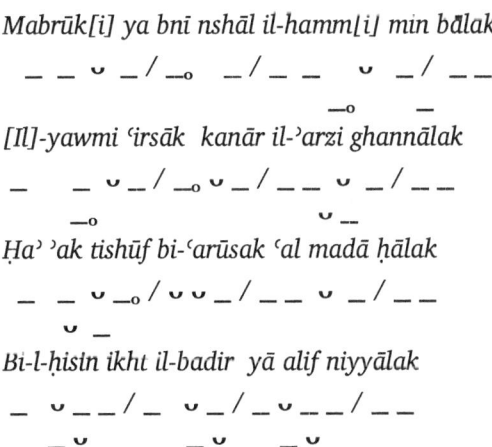

Recording 24: A recording by the author can be found at https://hdl.handle.net/20.500.12434/a07a4f76.

While the musical syllables differ slightly from the poetic syllables, reference to possible vernacular alternate readings of the poetic line will make the correspondence between poetic and musical syllables more precise. Leaving out *āyhā* from each hemistich, this is how the verse will scan poetically with variant readings indicated below the pertinent feet:

Mabrūk[i] ya bnī nshāl il-hamm[i] min bālak

– – ᴗ – / –o – / – – ᴗ – / – –

–o –

[Il]-yawmi ʿirsāk kanār il-ʾarzi ghannālak

– – ᴗ – / –o ᴗ – / – – ᴗ – / – –

–o ᴗ –

Ḥaʾ ʾak tishūf bi-ʿarūsak ʿal madā ḥālak

– – ᴗ –o / ᴗ ᴗ – / – – ᴗ – / – –

ᴗ –

Bi-l-ḥisin ikht il-badir yā alif niyyālak

– ᴗ – – / – ᴗ – / – ᴗ – – / – –

– ᴗ – ᴗ – ᴗ

Notwithstanding the substitution of _ _ ᴗ _ to _ ᴗ _ _, the scansion produces a standard *basīṭ* hemistich in each case: _ _ ᴗ _ / _ ᴗ _ / _ _ ᴗ _ / _ _. The *nathr*ish quality of *zalghaṭa* makes it difficult to seek perfect correspondence between the free accents of the musical lines and the stresses of the poetic line because musical transcriptions are ultimately concerned with the laws and rules of music. With reference, however, to the heard accents when the hemistichs are sung, the following stress pattern emerges:

_ _́ ᴗ _́ / _́o _́ / _ _́ ᴗ _́ / _ _́ / _́o _́
_ _́ ᴗ _́ / _́o ᴗ _́ / _ _́ ᴗ _́ / _ _́ / _́o ᴗ _
_ _́ ᴗ _́o / ᴗ́ ᴗ _́ / _ _́ ᴗ _́ / _ _́ / _́ _́
_ ᴗ́ _ _́ / _́ ᴗ _́ / _ ᴗ́ _ _́ / _ _́ / _́ ᴗ _́ ᴗ

This is the predominant stress pattern associated with the *basīṭ* metre. Add to this the regular appearance of short and long syllables in the order given to the *basīṭ fuṣḥā* metre and we have a quantitative proof that the metre is indeed that of *basīṭ*.

***

Abū al-zuluf, *al-shurūqī*, and *al-mawwāl al-baghdādī*. *Abū al-zuluf*, *al-shurūqī*, and *al-mawwāl al-baghdādī* are treated together here because all three are traditionally subsumed under Lebanese songs and because they belong in varying degrees to the *nathr* rather than the *naẓm* style. All three, moreover, exhibit a pattern of syllables resembling the *basīṭ fuṣḥā* metre. In each one of these three genres, the musical score reveals a freedom of accentuation typical of *nathr* pieces, but the music also preserves, to a great extent, the quantity of syllables that poetic scansion yields. In all, poetry dictates musical form, not vice versa.

Abū al-zuluf differs from the other two in that it is framed by a proto-tune consisting of the words: *Hayhāt-[i] yā buz-zuluf // ʿAynī yā mūlayyā* which cues the singer in a way similar to the *mījanā* proto-tune discussed earlier. The verse then ends with the same proto-tune in the last phrase of the last hemistich. The proto-tune is significant in another way. When its accented syllables are superimposed upon the poetic line, we get a clear idea which poetic syllables are stressed. The tension between poetic and linguistic stress notwithstanding, the analysis that follows makes clear that we are dealing with the *basīṭ fuṣḥā* metre.

Figure 26: *Abū al-zuluf*

Recording 25: A recording by the author can be found at https://hdl.handle.net/20.500.12434/18f75833.

The first musical phrase or motif, corresponding to the first poetic hemistich, has six beats preceded by an upbeat. It divides into three pairs of beats of equal length, the accented beats of these internal pairs corresponding with *hā yā* and *zū*.

The second phrase is shorter than the first, with the first of the three pairs of beats being truncated into one beat group. The accents which open each one of the groups correspond with *ʿay*, *mū*, *lay*. Or,

A	*Hay hāt [i] yā buz zū luf*
	— — ⏑ — — —[30] —
musical accent corresponds with	
	— —́ ⏑ —́ —́ —́ —́
B	*ʿAy nī ya mūlayyā*
	— — ⏑ — — —
musical accent corresponds with	
	—́ — ⏑ —́ —́ —́

When we take into consideration that linguistic, as opposed to poetic, stress in the foot — — ⏑ — would transpose the stress from the second long syllable to the first long one (— —́ ⏑ —́ —́ — ⏑ —́), which is precisely what obtains in the first foot of the second hemistich, and when we allow for a necessary shift in stress when the last short syllable of the first hemistich is given its length value as delivered (i.e., — ⏑ — — — —) with the ensuing dislocation and change of linguistic stress (—́ ⏑ —́ — —́ —), the resemblance with the *basīṭ* metre becomes easy to discern.

Bearing in mind the stress pattern of *abū al-zuluf* and its syllabic breakdown, it is important to note a few features which are elicited from sung versions of the genre. Lecerf, citing the text of an *abū al-zuluf* verse,[31] produces a transliteration which bears

---

[30] In A and B, syllable 6 may in some singing sound short (⏑), but in this case, syllable 7 will become extra-long: $—_{o}$.

[31] Lecerf 1932, 237.

little resemblance to the sung version. Here is, for example, the *maṭlaʿ* ('opening verse'), as he has it:

> *Haihāt! Yā Bū z-Zọlof ʿệnī yāmọ leyyä!*
> *Anwār luṯfak badat fī-lyāli ŝhatwiyyä*
>
> 'Comme c'est loin Abou Zolof mon aimé, (litt. mon œil) maman secours-moi'
> 'Les lumières de la douceur ont paru dans des nuit embrumées'
>
> (As Abou Zolof, my beloved [lit., my eye], is so far away, mother help me.)
> (The lights of sweetness have appeared in misty nights.)[32]

Even allowing for the Syrian and particularly Damascene pronunciation evident in the transliteration, the text, as it stands, scans as follows:

> _ _ _ _ _ _ _ _ _ _ _ _ _
> _ _ _ _ ᴗ _ _ _ _ _ _ _ _

Clearly, the lines as scanned have a hardly recognizable metre. Had Lecerf transliterated phonetically with reference to the tune, a number of short syllables would have appeared:

> *Hayhāt[i] yā bu z-zuluf ʿAynī ya mūlayyā*
> _ _ ᴗ _ / _ ᴗ _ / _ _ ᴗ _ / _ _
> *Anwār[i] luṯfak bādat fī lyālī shatwiyya*
> _ _ ᴗ _ / _ _ _ / _o _ _ _ / _ _

The second foot of both lines, which scans poetically as _ ᴗ _ undergoes, when sung, a lengthening of its second syllable. Also, the third foot of the second line is composed of _o _ _ _, rather than the familiar *basīṭ* foot _ _ ᴗ _. In this latter case, the reason is attributed to dialectal rather than musical exigencies. As these

---

[32] Lecerf 1932, 237.

changes affecting these particular feet are so frequent, it is necessary to anticipate them for the proper determination of metre.

In terms of line division and rhyme scheme, *abū al-zuluf* appears in two popular forms. In both, there is a *maṭlaʿ* and a *dawr* (i.e., 'main verse') which have one of the following two structures:

A)	*Maṭlaʿ*	___a	___a
	Dawr	___b	___b
		___b	___a
B)	*Maṭlaʿ*	___a	___b
		___c	___b
	Dawr	___c	___d
		___c	___d
		___c	___d
		___c	___b

Al-shurūqī (also *shrūqī*) or *al-qaṣīd al-badawī* ('the Bedouin *qaṣīd*') or *al-shammarī* (a *nisba* or relative adjective for the tribe of Shammar) is, as its name implies, a popular genre among the Bedouins in East Jordan and the eastern part of the Syrian desert. The Bedouins employ it in their wars and raids, and sing it, in the manner of the troubadours to the accompaniment of the *rabāb,* in the bazaars of towns and cities which they frequent for trading purposes.

The poem in *shurūqī,* called a *shrūqiyya,* is usually, but not necessarily, an extended narrative which treats of the heroic deeds of a central character, giving it an epic quality uncommon in *fuṣḥā* compositions. The metre used by the Bedouins, however, has little resemblance to the adaptations of *shurūqī* by the Lebanese *zajal* poets, and there is no room here to discuss the special dialectal and musical principles involved in the Bedouin prototype. What seems certain and more relevant to this study is that the Lebanese *zajjāls* have adapted the basic Bedouin melody to an altogether different metre, showing clear preference for love themes while retaining the basic rhyme scheme which consists of one rhyme for all the first hemistichs and another for all the second ones:

___a ___b
___a ___b
___a ___b
___a ___b etc.

Figure 27: *Shurūqī*

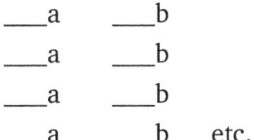

Yā mi ni ya tal ᶜal bi has bi-t kha fi fil ā lam - -
O my heart desire, would that you stilled the pain
Mā lidh dhit il ᶜaysh il lā - bil ha wā n nā mī
There's no pleasure in life except in love that grows
Mā hay ma nit rīh min fa ji rad du hāl bas sām - -
No breeze has wafted from the smiling dawn
Il lā li tun shur ᶜā lal ay yām as qā - - - - - mī - - - - -
except to [relate to the days] unfold my love sickness

Recording 26: A recording by the author can be accessed at https://hdl.handle.net/20.500.12434/18436656.

This is a *nathr* piece which exhibits, when scanned poetically, the kind of metrical uniformity which characterises modern compositions of *shurūqī*. Scansion based on sung verses of *shurūqī* produces a systematic alternation of feet, easily identifiable in *fuṣḥā* with the prevalent form of the *basīṭ* metre, as was the case with *abū al-zuluf*. The notation above preserves in large part the quantity of syllables. Short poetic syllables go with short notes or are joined with preceding long syllables and given the value of a musical long syllable. Long poetic syllables correspond either to a long or accented musical note or fall on triplet notes which have the capacity to correspond either to long or to short syllables.

The transcriptions of *abū al-zuluf* and *shurūqī* reveal that both genres are characterised by a regular beat, though only *abū al-zuluf* has an identifying musical metre in some parts. The fact that *abū al-zuluf* is framed by a proto-tune may explain this kind of rhythmic regularity, which puts *abū al-zuluf* somewhere between the *nathr* and *naẓm* styles. Another difference between the two genres is the more frequent appearance of triplet figures in *shurūqī* than in *abū al-zuluf*. This is important because triplet notes can be used for either long or short poetic syllables, and therefore can reflect more accurately (in the part governed by the proto-tune) poetic syllable quantity. Conversely, the low frequency of triplet figures in *abū al-zuluf* makes the musical metre the main determinant of musical duration. Despite these differences, the poetic metre of both genres seems easily adaptable to both tunes.

In order to ascertain this adaptability, the same text was given to Zaghlūl al-Dāmūr and he was asked to sing it to the *shurūqī* tune first and then to that of *abū al-zuluf*. He started out by singing the *abū al-zuluf* proto-tune. Then, with great ease, he gave a rendition of *shurūqī* and *abū al-zuluf* respectively.

Figure 28: Proto-tune

Here again, despite the difficulty of obtaining a perfect correspondence between the musical accents and the stress pattern of *basīṭ*, the short poetic syllables always correspond to short musical notes, thus preserving the formal quantitative pattern of the *basīṭ* metre.

Al-mawwāl al-baghdādī shares these same characteristics of the two genres discussed above. Its *nathr*ish quality makes determination of poetic stress difficult but syllable quantity is faithfully preserved in the musical score. Here is, for example, a phonetic transliteration of the two verses transcribed musically below:

Yā maʿshara n-nās[i] mā bi-d-dahir ṣāḥib wafī

_ _ ⏑ _ / _ ⏑ _/ _ ⏑ _ _/ _ ⏑ _

_ ⏑

'O people, there is no faithful friend in life (the world)'

Mallayt[i] ḥatta nbarā minnī lisānī wa-fī

_ _ ⏑ _/ _ ⏑ _/ _ _ ⏑ _/ _ ⏑ _

'I got bored until both my mouth and tongue became worn out'

Allowing for the repetition of *Yā maʿshara-n-nās* twice in the musical notation, and allowing for the short vowel *i* after the extra-long syllables *nās* and *layt* (in *Mallayt*), the poetic scansion yields a standard *basīṭ*, with all the short syllables corresponding with short notes. In the case of *nās*, however, the music gives it, the first time around, the value of a quarter note (♩), but this is so because the short poetic syllable *i* is joined with the preceding syllable forming together a quarter note (♩). Otherwise, the transcription reflects accurately the quantity of poetic syllable structure.

Figure 29: *Al-mawwāl al-baghdādī*

Recording 27: A recording by the author can be found at https://hdl.handle.net/20.500.12434/8dde3b55.

The scansion of a large number of recorded samples of *al-mawwāl al-baghdādī* shows two slightly different configurations of the *basīṭ* metre, either _ _ ⏑ _ / _ ⏑ _ / _ _ ⏑ _ / _ ⏑ _ or _ _ ⏑ _ / _ ⏑ _ / _ _ ⏑ _ / _ _, with the last foot changing from _ ⏑ _

to _ _, which is a legitimate alternative in the rules of *fuṣḥā* metrics. Unfortunately, this fact is lost on Whaybeh who assumes that each hemistich must have fourteen syllables[33] and therefore that the metre of *al-mawwāl al-baghdādī* must be *al-mutawāzī* which his system characterises by fourteen syllables. At any rate, the example that Whaybeh cites[34] consists of seven hemistichs, the first three and the seventh of which contain fourteen syllables each, but the fourth, fifth and sixth have only thirteen each.

Although the designation *mawwāl* seems to be part of the name of this genre of *zajal*, the poets and aficionado of *zajal* use the term with reference to *ʿatābā, mījanā, shurūqī* and *abū al-zuluf* as well. A poet is usually asked to sing a *mawwāl* of *ʿatābā* or *mījanā* or any one of the others. While the *mawwāl* can be sung by itself, it is generally rendered in the middle of a popular song, as a variation on the basic tune of that particular song.

The term *mawwāl* itself has an interesting origin. It derives, most probably, from *mawāliyā*, one of *al-funūn al-sabʿa* ('the seven arts') which were not always the same seven that the various classical authorities had enumerated. Whether or not the term was related to *al-mawālī* ('the non-Arab Muslims') is highly problematic. Of more relevance perhaps is the possibility that *mawwāl* was originally used as the name of a singer of *mawāliyā* and then reverted to the name of the song itself.[35]

---

33 Whaybeh 1952, 80.

34 Whaybeh 1952, 80.

35 See Whaybeh 1952, 56–57.

Like *ʿatābā* and *mījanā, al-mawwāl al-baghdādī* employs homonyms at the ends of hemistichs, but its structure is usually more complex. A typical *mawwāl baghdādī* consists of seven hemistichs with two sets of homonyms, one for the first three and the seventh and one for the fourth, fifth and sixth hemistichs:

___ homonym A	___ homonym A
___ homonym A	___ homonym B
___ homonym B	___ homonym B

___ homonym A

***

Mkhammas mardūd. As we have argued above, the main metre in the *naẓm* style is the *qarrādī* metre, which has a strict rhythmic pattern imposed by a musical metre, producing a neutral realization of the following trochaic pattern ´_ _ ´_ _ ´_ _ ´_ with a wide variety of internal and external rhyme schemes and strophic divisions.

Al-mukhammas al-mardūd (or *mkhammas mardūd*) is a very popular *qarrādī* composition used in verbal duels and other *zajal* occasions, primarily for psychological and sometimes comic relief and as a means of establishing the poets' credentials with their audiences. While its rhyming phrases along with the repetition and reversal of word order allow for audience participation, its simple but ornate musical rendition facilitates this participation and establishes a psychological space, a relief from the heated verbal arguments preceding and succeeding it. A typical *mkhammas mardūd* consists of a four-hemistich *maṭlaʿ* ('proem-refrain or overture') rhyming a b, a b or a a, b a and a nine-hemistich *dawr* (or *simṭ*):

Example A *maṭlaʿ* a a, b a
dawr c d, c d, c d, c e, a
Example B *maṭlaʿ* a b, a b
dawr c d, c d, c d, c e, b

Example A

Maṭlaʿ إلعامِل حالو مْنِ الأبطال \\ مين قَلّلو عَ السّاحة نْزال

ʾIl-ʿāmil ḥālu mni l-ʾabṭāl // Mīn ʾallu ʿa s-sāḥa nzāl
'He who considers himself a hero //
who asked him to descend on the arena?'

بَدنا بالزِّندِ المفتول \\ نْشيلِ القَيمِة الماب تِنشال

Badnā bi-z-zindi l-maftūl // Nshīl il-ʾaymi l-mab tinshāl
'We want (someone) with muscles to //
Lift the weight that cannot be lifted'

Dawr بْزَقفة كَفّ بْنينا أَساس \\ وْعَ المتراسِ الشَّملِ التَّفّ

B-zaʾfit kaffi bnayna ʾsās // W-ʿa l-mitrās ish-shamli ltaff
'With a (mere) clap we laid the foundation' //
'And on the battle front the friends met'

التَّفّ الشَّملِ عَ المتراس \\ بْنينا أَساسِ بْزَقفِة كَفّ

Iltaff ishamli ʿla l-mitrās // Bnayna ʾsāsi b-zaʾfit kaff
'The friends met on the battle front' //
'We laid the foundation with a (mere) clap'

بْدَفّ وْمِوّالَين وْكاس \\ قْبالِ النّاسِ وْقِفنا صَفّ

Bdaff iw-miwwālayn iw-kās // ʾBāli n-nāsi w-ʾifna ṣaff
'With one tambourine, two *mawwāls* and one drink' //
'In front of the crowds we stood in a line'

صَفِّ وْقِفنا قْبالِ النّاس \\ بْمِوّالِ وْكاسِ وْدَفّين

Ṣaffi wʾifna ʾbāl in-nās // B-miwwāl iw-kās iw-daffayn
'In a line we stood in front of the crowds' //
'With one *mawwāl*, one cup and two tambourines'

وْدَفٍّ وْكاسَينِ وْمِوّال

W-daff iw-kāsayn iw-miwwāl
'And one tambourine, two cups and one *mawwāl*'

Example B

Maṭlaʿ ساحتنا مَلعَبْ لِلخيل \\ وْجَوقِتنا قَلعِة أشعار

Sāḥitnā malʿab li-l-khayl // W-jawʾitnā ʾlʿit ashʿār
'Our arena is a playground for horses' //
'And our troupe is a citadel for poetry'

مِبنِيِّة عَ جْناحِ الليل \\ بْكِلمِة نورِ وْكِلمِة نار

Mibniyyi ʿa jnāḥ il-layl // B-kilmit nūri w-kilmit nār
'Erected on night's wings' //
'With words of light and words of fire'

Dawr لما النّهرِ زْرَعتو دْياب \\ شَعرو شابِ وْخاف الدَّهر

Lamma n-nahr izraʿtu dyāb // Shaʿrū shāb iw-khāf id-dahr
'When in the river I planted wolves' //
'Its hair grew white, and fate was scared'

خافِ الدَّهرِ وْشَعرو شاب \\ لما دْيابِ زْرَعتِ النَّهر

Khāfi d-dahri w-shaʿrū shāb // Lamma dyābi zraʿti n-nahr
'Fate was scared, and its hair grew white' //
'When wolves I planted in the river'

بْلَوحِ وْمِسمارينِ وْباب \\ سَبع اِلغابِ حْبَستو شَهر

Blawḥi w-mismārayni w-bāb // Sabʿ il-ghābi ḥbastū shahr
'With one board, two nails and one door' //
'The lion of the jungle I imprisoned one whole month'

حْبَستو شهرِ لسَبعِ الغاب \\ بْمِسمارِ وْبابَين وْلَوح

Ḥbastū shahri l-sabʿi l-ghāb // B-mismāri w-bābayni w-lawḥ
'I imprisoned for a whole month the lion of the jungle'//
'With one nail, two doors, and one board'

وْلَوحينِ وْبابِ وْمِسمار

W-lawḥayni w-bābi w-mismār
'And two boards, one door, and one nail'

Several features are apparent in the two examples above. With specific reference to Example A, the nine-hemistich *dawr* consists of two major divisions. The first four hemistichs break into phrases or clauses, two per hemistich, with the following internal rhyme: a′ b′ // b′ a′, c′ b′ // b′ a′

Example A

Bzaʾfit kaff	*bnay-naʾ-sās*	*W ʿal-mitrās*	*ish-sham-l-il-taff*
a′	b′	b′	a′
Iltaff-ishamli	*ʿ-lal-mitrās*	*Bnay-naʾ-sās*	*b-zaʾfit kaff*
c′	b′	b′	a′

Each phrase or clause is further divided into two words: a': 1) *zaʾfit* and 2) *kaff*; b': 1) *bnay-na* and 2) *ʾsās*; b': 1) *ʿlā* and 2) *mitrās*; a': 1) *shaml* and 2) *il-taff*; c': 1) *il-taff* and 2) *shaml*; b': 1) *ʿlā* and 2) *mitrās*; b': 1) *bnay-na* and 2) *ʾsās*; and a': 1) *zaʾfit* and 2) *kaff*, altogether adding up to 16. When the words are numbered in order from 1 to 16, the following internal rhymes obtain: 1/15, 2/8/9/16, 3/13, 4/6/12/14, 5/11.

Example A

Bzaʾfit	*kaff*	*bnayna*	*ʾsās*	*W-ʿal*	*mitrās*	*ish-shaml*	*iltaff*
1	2	3	4	5	6	7	8
Iltaff	*ish-shaml*	*ʿ-lal*	*mitrās*	*Bnayna*	*ʾsās*	*bzaʾfit*	*kaff*
9	10	11	12	13	14	15	16

In addition to this mosaic of rhyming words, phrases, and clauses, there is a clear transposition of the words in clauses a′ and c′, *shaml* and *iltaff* versus *iltaff* and *shaml*. The rest of the clauses are repeated without transposition.

Involved as these divisions and subdivisions are, they are predictable and thus enable the educated *zajal* audiences to become actual participants in the song.

The second major division consists of the last five hemistichs in the *dawr*.

{Bdaff-iw-miwwālay-niw-kās} // *{ʾBā-lin-nā-siw-ʾif-na ṣaff}*
1 2
{Ṣaff-iw-ʾif-naʾ-bā lin-nās} // *{Bmiwwāl-iw-kās-iw-daffayn}*
3 4
{Wdaff-iw kāsayn-iw-miwwāl}
5

(Within the whole *dawr*, these are hemistichs 5, 6, 7, 8, 9.)

This time around audience participation is further encouraged by predictable strategies of a slightly different kind. Three words are introduced in hemistich number 5, two in the singular and one in dual form: one *daff*, two *miwwāls*, and one *kās*. These words then go through a different sort of transposition in hemistichs 8 and 9, with *daff* in 5 appearing in dual form at the end of 8 and with *kās* in 5 becoming *kāsayn* in dual form in 9. It is important for one of the words in 5 to rhyme in its singular form with rhyme *a* of the *maṭlaʿ*. Thus *miwwālayn* (dual, two *miwwāls*) or *miwwāl* (in singular form) rhymes perfectly with *a* of the *maṭlaʿ*. Hemistichs 6 and 7 repeat the internal rhymes of the previous four hemistichs (but not the actual words) and the transpositions that take place in hemistichs 2 and 3 of the first major division of the *dawr*.

While such complicated features suggest a great deal of deliberateness and artificiality on the part of the oral poet, they nevertheless enable the accomplished poet to improvise, precisely because the genre has a clearly delineated structure and a relatively small number of rhyming words, phrases, and clauses.

The etymology of the name *mukhammas mardūd* presents a problem. *Mukhammas* suggests that we are dealing with quintuples, arrangements of lines or metrical units in fives, but nothing on the level of structure or metrical feet allows for the nomenclature of this genre. The *maṭlaʿ* consists of four hemistichs, not five, each of which is rendered with four distinct musical beats and four stressed poetic syllables. The *dawr* follows the same poetic stress pattern as the *maṭlaʿ*, and the rhyme schemes of both the *maṭlaʿ* and the *dawr* cannot be grouped into quinary systems or arrangements. Anṭūn ʿAkkārī claims that

> *Al-mukhammas al-mardūd* refers to any *zajal* composition whose *maṭlaʿ* is comprised of four hemistichs and whose *dawr* has been quintupled by responding to (or returning to) the third hemistich. This is the derivation of the terms *mukhammas* and *mardūd*. It (this method) can be found in the various genres of colloquial poetry such as the *maʿannā*, the *qarrādī*, the *qaṣīd*—both short and long varieties—and other (genres).[36]

This bewildering statement does not accord with the huge number of *mukhammas mardūd* compositions available in print and on tape throughout Lebanon and clearly identified by poets as *mukhammas mardūd*. How the *dawr* is 'quintupled' by returning to the third hemistich (of the *dawr*, one would suppose) is not made clear. Nor does ʿAkkārī offer a specific example. The two examples above bear no such claim. As to ʿAkkārī's statement that *mukhammas mardūd* may be 'found' in *maʿannā* and *qaṣīd* compositions, I have yet to see one such example, except perhaps that some *maʿannā* and *qaṣīd* compositions, and there is ample proof to such a claim, may employ the kind of repetition and transpositions discussed above as formal features of *mukhammas mardūd*.

---

[36] ʿAkkārī 1986, 49.

It seems to me that ʿAkkārī, like other Lebanese writers on *zajal*, confuses genre with rhyme schemes and other poetic features.

Still, where does the name come from? Since *mukhammas mardūd* is sung to a strict musical tune, part of the answer, at least, should be sought in music. As the musical transcription below makes clear, it is highly probable that the early singers of *mukhammas mardūd* were speaking in musical terms of the musical return (*da capo*) of the last hemistich (9) in the *dawr*, to the *maṭlaʿ*. This explains the term *mardūd* (literally 'that which is returned to'). As for the word *mukhammas*, it is equally probable that the 'quintupling' sense of the word refers to the fifth hemistich of the second major division of the *dawr* (hemistichs 5, 6, 7, 8 and 9) which initiates the play on the three words *daff*, *miwwālayn*, and *kās*. In this second division hemistich 5 (or 9 in the *dawr*) ends the play on words begun in hemistich 5 of the whole *dawr* or hemistich 1 of the second major division. In other words, the fifth hemistich of the second division returns to the fifth hemistich of the whole *dawr*. When I presented this explanation to Tawfiq Abdo, a well-known *zajal* poet, he admitted that he composed his *mukhammas mardūd* pieces with precisely this explanation in the back of his mind, but that he could not express it in words.

When the *mukhammas mardūd* is introduced in a verbal duel or a less formal occasion, a poet sings the *maṭlaʿ* and follows it with his *dawr*. The chorus and the audience take their cue from the last hemistich in the *dawr* and sing the *maṭlaʿ* again. Another poet then introduces his own *dawr*, ending it with a rhyme that 'returns' to that of the *maṭlaʿ*, and so on. While the various *dawrs* vary their rhyme schemes, the transpositions in the second division are executed in the same manner and the last word in the *dawr* is made to rhyme with the last word of the *maṭlaʿ*.

Clearly such artificial word-transposition is not conducive to verbal duelling in the strict sense of the phrase, the emphasis being on wordplay in *mukhammas mardūd* rather than on theme and topic. However, since the poet's strategy in a verbal duel is to prevail in an argument, it is important for the poet to establish rapport with the audience by demonstrating his or her knowledge of rhyme and wordplay. Moreover, if the poet has a good voice in singing, this can only earn him or her points in the context of the whole duel.

The musical transcription below is of a popular song by Fayrouz, Lebanon's most famous female singer, and her male counterpart Nasri Shamsiddin. As part of a longer operetta entitled 'A Love Poem', it is intended, in my opinion, as a musical ornamentation to highlight the theme of love in the operetta. It is chosen here because the sophisticated music accompanying it represents clearly the beats, accents and ornaments employed in live *zajal* performances and because the *dawr*s that follow exhibit slight variations in form and length, typical of musical adaptations of *zajal* genres.

Figure 30: *Mkhammas mardūd*[37]

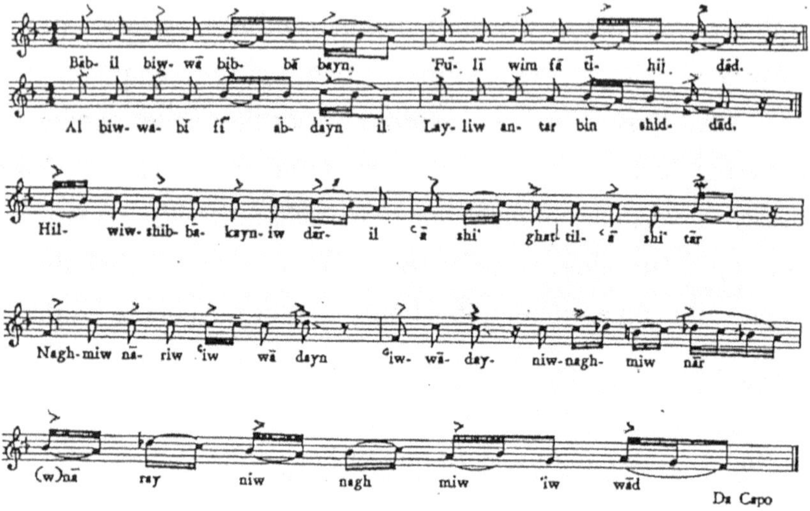

Recording 28: A recording by the author can be accessed at https://hdl.handle.net/20.500.12434/a172c611.

The *maṭlaʿ*, or choral refrain, resembles the standard *maṭlaʿ* of the previous two examples. The *dawr*, however, is rendered in five hemistichs, the first and third of which introduce two different sets of three-word phrases. Hemistich 3 initiates the word-transposition-play familiar in *mukhammas mardūd* compositions. The *dawrs* that follow consist of five hemistichs each and repeat the form of the first *dawr*, except for the second *dawr* which initiates the three-word transposition in hemistich 3 only:

[37] Music was transcribed by Professor Manny Rubin, Professor of Music at the University of Massachusetts, Amherst. A video clip can be found here: https://youtu.be/BXvyNfws3uY?si=QRdq9P9u8TIsdig3.

Fayrouz

Maṭlaʿ باب البِوّابة بْبابَين \\ قْفولِة وِمفْاتيح جْداد

Bāb il-biwwābbi b-bābayn // ʾFūli wi-mfātīḥ ijdād
'The gate consists of two doors' // 'locks and new keys'

عَ البِوّابِة في عَبدَين \\ إللَّيلِ وْعَنتَر بِن شِدّاد

ʿAl biwwābi fī ʿabdayn // il-layli w-ʿAntar Bin Shiddād
'At the gate there are two black (men, things)' //
'The night and Antar Bin Shaddad'

حِلوِة وْشِبّاكَين وْدار \\ العاشِق غَطِّ العاشِق طار

Ḥilwi w-shibbākayn iw-dār // Lʿāshiʾ ghaṭṭ il-ʿāshiʾ ṭār
'One pretty girl, two windows and one house' //
'The lover alights, the lover flies off'

نَغمِة وْنارِ وْعِوّادَين \\ عِوّادَينِ وْنَغمِة وْنار

Naghm iw-nār iw-ʿiwwādayn // ʿIwwādayn iw-naghm iw-nār
'One tune, one fire, and two oud players' //
'Two oud players, one tune and one fire'

وْنارَين وْنَغمِة وْعِوّاد

W-nārayn iw-naghm iw-ʿiwwād
'Two fires, a tune and an oud player'
(*maṭlaʿ* repeated)

Nasri

يا حِلوِة اللّي ريفِك رَفّ \\ بْتِمشي وْخَلفِك يِمشي الصَّفّ

Yā ḥilwi llī rīfik raff // Btimshi w-khalfik yimshi ṣ-ṣaff
'O, pretty one with fluttering eyelashes' //
'You walk and people queue up behind you'

دَفّ وْكَفّ وْرِدّادَين \\ رِدّادَينِ وْدَفّ وْكَفّ

Daff iw-kaff iw-riddādayn // Riddādayn iw-daff iw-kaff
'One tambourine, one palm (of hand) and two chorus
members' // 'Two chorus members, one
tambourine, one palm'

وْكَفَّينِ وْدَفِّ وْرِدّاد

Wkaffayn iw-daff iw-riddād

'Two palms, one tambourine and a chorus member'

(*maṭlaʿ* repeated)

Fayrouz

صَحرا وْقافِلتَينِ وْخَيل \\ العَتمِة مَيلِ النِجمِة مَيل

Ṣaḥra w-ʾāfiltayn iw-khayl // L-ʿatmi mayl in-nijmi mayl

'One desert, two caravans and horses' //

'Darkness on one side, the star on the other'

فَحمِ وْلَيلِ وْحِدّادَين \\ حِدّادَينِ وْفَحمِ وْلَيل

Faḥm iw-layl iw-ḥiddādayn // Ḥiddādayn iw-faḥm iw-layl

'Charcoal, a night, and two blacksmiths' //

'Two blacksmiths, charcoal and night'

وْلَيلَينِ وْفَحمِ وْحِدّاد

W-laylayn iw-faḥm iw-ḥiddād

'Two nights, charcoal and one blacksmith'

(*maṭlaʿ* repeated)

Nasri

خَوخِ وْرِمّانِ وْصِبَّير \\ يْمَسّيكُن يا أهلِ الخَير

Khawkh iw-rimmān iw-ṣibbayr // Ymassīkun yā ahl il-khayr

'Plums, pomegranate and cactus' //

'I bid you good evening, good people'

جِفتِ وْطَيرِ وْصِيّادَين \\ صِيّادَينِ وْجِفتِ وْطَير

Jift iw-ṭayr iw-ṣiyyādayn // Ṣiyyādayn iw-jift iw-ṭayr

'One shotgun, one bird and two hunters' //

'Two hunters, one shotgun and one bird'

وْطَيرَينِ وْجِفتِ وْصِيّاد

Wṭayrayn iw-jift iw-ṣiyyād

'Two birds, one shotgun and one hunter'

(*maṭlaʿ* repeated)

The unifying theme of these vignettes is love. The power of suggestion is managed here in words resembling idiograms, that allow the audience to write out, as it were, the various love scenes, without the intervention of logical connections and narrative sequence. The same power of suggestion is evident in Examples A and B above, except that in those examples the theme is that of boasting and vainglory. In all cases, *mukhammas mardūd* compositions invite audience participation, by enabling the audience to partake in the creative act of composition.

In terms of the overall musical structure, this is a professional rendition of a folk melody and text, which shows sophisticated adaptation of folk material for modern performance. The song consists of a refrain and *dawr*s, sung by Fayrouz and Nasri as alternating soloists followed by choral rendition of the refrain preceding and succeeding each *dawr*. Variations and melodic excursions are introduced for each new *dawr* to avoid literal repetition. However, the melodic material remains basically the same throughout the song even though some of the variants add extra measures or modify key structural pitches.

The rhythmic activity of each *dawr* increases toward its end. Each phrase ends with a brief downward flurry of motion that mirrors the same idea in miniature, imparting a sense of structural cohesiveness to the whole.

Structurally the refrain consists of two phrases (transcribed above as full 4/4 measures) combined in a question–answer (antecedent–consequent) format into a two-measure phrase which is then repeated. The pulse is regular and strongly marked. The structure of the verse, on the other hand, is extended in its fifth measure, corresponding to the fifth poetic phrase. This may account for the allusion to 'five' (*mukhammas*) in the name of the genre. Moreover, there is the sense that the last line of the music 'returns' without stopping, or breathing; it 'falls into' the refrain without pause.

The musical accents coincide with the beats, heavy accents fall on the poetic syllables 1, 3, 5, 7 and produce a typical *qarrādī* metre. This coincidence characterises all poetry in the *naẓm* style, where the music writes the poetry. The musical formula is ready-made, and the poet's function is to fill the formula with words, observing the strict trochaic pattern imposed by the musical metre. Finally, because the musical metre is essential to the composition, writing the poetry as it does and dislocating poetic and natural stress patterns, it ceases to be language-specific.

CONCLUSION

This book has journeyed through the vibrant world of Lebanese *zajal*, exploring its rich traditions, intricate metrics, and cultural significance. The Introduction's nostalgic recounting of a 1958 *zajal* event sets the stage for an in-depth study of this cherished form of oral poetry. *Zajal*, with its competitive poetic duels and communal performances, is more than a cultural pastime; it is a dynamic expression of Lebanese identity and creativity, deeply embedded in the country's social fabric and diaspora communities.

Chapter One laid the groundwork by defining key terms and establishing a methodological framework for analysing the metrics of *zajal*. This chapter highlighted the critical role of music and chorus in proper scansion, emphasizing the inclusion of stress in analysis—an aspect often overlooked in earlier studies.

A review of existing scholarship followed in Chapter Two, highlighting the contributions and limitations of previous critical approaches. Much of the existing criticism is marred by impressionistic statements, contradictions, and a notable lack of documentation. Crucially, the absence of music, song, and stress in earlier metrical studies was noted, setting the stage for a more comprehensive approach.

The relationship between *fuṣḥā* and *zajal* meters was explored in Chapter Three, illustrating how certain *zajal* meters are derived from classical *fuṣḥā* meters. Through a case study of an early *zajal* by Sulaymān al-Ashlūḥī, key meters like *al-rajaz*, *al-ramal*, and *al-basīṭ* were identified, posing important questions

 https://doi.org/10.11647/OBP.0424.07

about their quantitative, qualitative, syllabic, and stress-based characteristics.

Chapter Four delved into the role of stress in both *fuṣḥā* Arabic verse and *zajal*, identifying two musical styles—*nathr al-naghamāt* and *naẓm al-naghamāt*. An original methodology for scanning *maʿannā* and *qarrādī* pieces was developed, creating a framework that superimposes musical stress on poetic stress.

The *qarrādī* genre was explored in depth in Chapter Five, tracing its development from Maronite hymns and folk poetry to its contemporary forms. Musical transcriptions and analyses of various styles were included, drawing connections to Hispano-Arabic prototypes, and showcasing the genre's rich diversity.

Finally, Chapter Six focused on the musical transcription and scansion of popular genres such as *ʿatābā* and *mījanā*, alongside forms like the *qaṣīd*, *al-ḥidā*, and *al-mawwāl al-baghdādī*. This chapter demonstrated the use of oral-formulaic strategies by poets and highlighted the intricate relationship between musical meter and linguistic stress patterns.

The study concludes that a comprehensive understanding of *zajal* requires a holistic approach that integrates music, stress, and the role of the chorus (*riddādeh*). These elements are essential for accurately describing the metrics of Lebanese *zajal* poetry. The methodologies developed in this research not only deepen the appreciation of *zajal* but also provide valuable tools for analysing other oral traditions.

In closing, Lebanese *zajal* stands as a testament to the enduring power of oral poetry. It is a living tradition that bridges the past and present, connecting communities through shared language and music. By situating Lebanese *zajal* within the broader landscape of Arabic and Mediterranean oral traditions, this book honours the creativity and resilience of poets who continue to enrich this vibrant cultural heritage. Looking ahead, this study aims to inspire further exploration and appreciation of the intricate artistry behind Lebanese *zajal* and its place in the world of oral literature.

REFERENCES

ʿAbbūd, Mārūn. 1968. *al-Shiʿr al-ʿāmmī*. Beirut: Dār al-Thaqāfa.

Abdel-Nour, Jabbour. 1957. *Étude sur la poésie dialectale au Liban*. Beirut: l'Université Libanaise.

Abū Dīb, Kamāl. 1974. *Fī al-bunya al-ʾīqāʿiyya li-l-shiʿr al-ʿarabī: Naḥwa badīl jadhrī li-ʿarūḍ al-Khalīl*. Beirut: Dār al-ʿIlm li-l-Malāyīn.

ʿAkkārī, Anṭūn. 1986. *al-Ashʿār al-shaʿbiyya al-lubnāniyya*. Tripoli (Lebanon): Jarrous Press.

al-Bustānī, Buṭruṣ. 1870. *Muḥīṭ al-muḥīṭ*. Beirut: Maktabat Lubnān.

al-Fighālī, Asʿad al-Khūrī. 1939. *Dīwān rāṣid al-maʿannā shaḥrūr al-wādī*. Kfarshima: Khāṣ Lubnān.

al-Ḥillī. 1983. *Dīwān Safiyy al-Dīn al-Ḥillī*. Beirut: Dār Ṣādir li-l-Ṭibāʿa wa-l-Nashr.

al-Hūrānī, Ibrāhīm. 1906. 'Lamḥa fī al-shiʿr, al-faṣīḥ wa al-ʿāmmī minhu'. *al-Nashra al-usbūʿiyya* 2121: 602–4.

al-Ibshīhī. 1900. *al-Mustaṭraf fī kull fann mustaẓraf*. Beirut: Dār Maktabat al Ḥayāt.

al-Jumayyil, Buṭruṣ. 1982. *Zajaliyyāt Jibrāʾīl Ibn al-Qilāʿī*. Beirut: Dār Laḥd Khāṭir.

al-Muḥibbī. 1873. *Khulāṣat al-athar fī aʿyān al-qarn al-ḥādī ʿashar*. 4 vols. Cairo: al-Maṭbaʿa al-Wahība.

ʿAwwād, Tawfīq. 1930. 'al-Shiʿr al-ʿāmmī'. *al-Mashriq* 28: 436–43, 501–8.

Brockelmann, Carl. 1928. *Lexicon Syriacum*. 2nd edition. Halle: Max Niemeyer.

Burgess, Henry. 1853. *Select Metrical Hymns and Homilies of Ephraem Syrus*. London: Blackader.

Cachia, Pierre. 1977. 'The Egyptian *Mawwāl*: Its Ancestry, Its Development, and Its Present Forms'. *Journal of Arabic Literature* 8: 77–103.

Corriente, Federico. 1980. *Gramática, métrica, y texto del cancionero hispanoárabe de Aban Quzmán*. Madrid: Instituto Hispano-Arabe de Cultura.

Dalmann, Gustaf H. 1901. *Palästinischer Diwan*. Leipzig: J. C. Hinrichs.

Dozy, Reinhart P. A. 1967. *Supplément aux dictionnaires arabes*. 2 vols. Leiden: Brill and Paris: Maisonneuve et Larose.

Frayḥa, Anīs. 1957. *Ḥaḍāra fī ṭarīq al-zawāl: al-qarya al-lubnāniyya*. Beirut: American University of Cairo.

———. 1973. *Muʿjam al-alfāẓ al-ʿāmiyya*. Beirut: Maktabat Lubnān.

García Gómez, Emilio. 1972. *Todo Ben Quzmān, editado, interpretado, medido y explicado*. 3 vols. Madrid: Gredos.

Hartmann, Martin. 1897. *Das arabische Strophengedicht I: Das Muwaššaḥ*. Weimar: Felber.

Haydar, Adnan. 1989. 'The Development of Lebanese *Zajal*: Genre, Meter, and Verbal Duel'. *Oral Tradition* 4 (1–2): 189–212.

Ibn Khaldûn. 1969. *The Muqaddimah: An Introduction to History*. Translated by Franz Rosenthal. Princeton, NJ: Princeton University Press.

Ibn Manẓūr. 1994. *Lisān al-ʿArab*. 18 vols. Beirut: Dār Ṣādir lil-Ṭibāʿa wa-al-Nashr.

Jayyusi, Salma Khadra. 1977. *Trends and Movements in Modern Arabic Poetry*. 2 vols. Leiden: Brill.

Kafrkadī, Naṣūr Ibrāhīm. 1942. *Sabk al-maʿānī fī al-zajal al-lubnānī*. 2 vols. Boston: The Syrian Press.

Kurpershoek, Marcel. 1994–2005. *Oral Poetry and Narratives from Central Arabia*. 5 vols. Leiden: Brill.

Lane, Edward William. 1984. *Arabic–English Lexicon*. 2 vols. London: Islamic Texts Society.

Lecerf, Jean. 1932. 'Littérature dialectale et renaissance arabe moderne'. *Bulletin d'études orientales* 2 (2): 179–258.

Littmann, Enno. 1902. *Neuarabische Volkspoesie*. Berlin: Weidmannsche Buchhandlung.

Lord, Albert B. 1960. *The Singer of Tales*. Cambridge, Mass.: Harvard University Press.

Monroe, James T. 1974. 'Preface and Introduction'. In *Hispano-Arabic Poetry: A Student Anthology*. Berkeley, Los Angeles and London: University of California Press.

———. 1975. 'Formulaic Diction and the Common Origins of Romance Lyric Traditions'. *Hispanic Review* 4: 341–50.

———. 1977. 'Studies on the *Ḫarǧas*: The Arabic and the Romance *Ḫarǧas*'. *Viator: Medieval and Renaissance Studies* 8:95–126.

———. 1989. 'Which Came First, the *Zajal* or the *Muwashshaḥa*? Some Evidence for the Oral Origins of Hispano-Arabic Strophic Poetry'. *Oral Tradition* 4 (1–2): 38–64.

Monroe, James T. and David Swialto. 1977. 'Ninety-Three Arabic *Ḫarǧas* in Hebrew *Muwaššaḥs*: Their Hispano-Romance

Prosody and Thematic Features'. *Journal of the American Oriental Society* 97 (2): 141–63.

Nakhleh, Amīn. 1945. *Maʿannā Rashīd Nakhleh*. Beirut: Maṭbaʿat al-Kashshāf.

Salāma, Būlus. 1962. *Ḥikāyat ʿumr*. Beirut: Maktabat al-Madrasa wa-Dār al-Kitāb al-Lubnānī.

Sowayan, Saad Abdullah. 1985. *Nabati Poetry: The Oral Poetry of Arabia*. Berkeley and Los Angeles, Calif.: University of California Press.

Weil, Gotthold. 1986. 'ʿArūḍ'. In *Encyclopaedia of Islam*, 2nd edition, edited by H. A. R. Gibb et al., I:667–677. Leiden: Brill.

Whaybeh, Munīr Ilyās. 1952. *al-Zajal: tārīkhuhu, adabuhu, aʿlāmuhu, qadīman wa ḥadīthan*. Ḥarīṣā: al-Maṭbaʿa al-Būlusiyya.

Zaydān, Jirjī. 1957. *Tārīkh ādāb al-lugha al-ʿarabiyya*, 4 vols. Cairo: Dār al-Hilāl.

INDEX

Abbasid, 14
ʿAbbūd, Mārūn, 35
Abdel-Nour, Jabbour, 19 n. 23, 56–60, 98–99, 127, 142–44, 154–57
Abdo, Tawfiq, 186
Abrahamī, Elia, 152
abū al-zuluf, 50, 55, 58, 170–72, 174, 176, 179
Abū Dīb, Kamāl, 21, 73–75, 95
ʿaddiyya, *See* counting rhymes
Afrāmiyyāt, 103–7, 113
Ajami, Mansour, 79–80, 86–87, 89, 116 n. 20, 139, 159 n. 27
ʿAkkārī, Anṭūn, 185–86
ʿalā dalʿūnā, 76
al-Akhfash, 61, 157 n. 24
al-alifiyyāt, 29
al-Andalus, 5
al-Ashlūḥī, Sulaymān, 69, 193
al-aswānī, 42, 45–46, 50–52, 60
al-badāli, 28–29
al-Bustānī, Buṭrus, 32
al-dubeit, 3
al-Faruqi, Lois, 77, 116 n. 20, 162
al-Ghazīrī, Elias, 106
al-Hāshim, Joseph, 17 n. 20, 53, 145. *See also* Zaghlūl al-Dāmūr
al-ḥasja, 3
al-ḥawraba, 30 n. 20, 165–66
al-ḥidā, 50, 53–54, 58–59, 109, 111, 154–58, 161, 166, 194
al-Ḥillī, Ṣafiyy al-Dīn, 27
al-Ḥūrānī, Ibrāhīm, 19 n. 23, 33–35, 38
al-Ibshīhī, 27, 29
al-kān wa-kān, 27
al-Khalīl, 14, 18, 20–21, 28, 32, 35–36, 38, 41, 43, 58–59, 61, 66 n. 5, 67, 72–74, 76, 79, 87, 93–95, 97–100, 127, 141, 144–45, 157 n. 24
al-malḥūn, 3
al-marṣūd, 29
al-maṭlaʿ, 28, 30 n. 18, 36, 144, 173–74, 180–82, 184–90
al-mawāliyyāt, 27
al-mawwāl al-baghdādī, 31, 50, 55, 170, 177–80, 194
al-maʿṣūb, 136, 140
al-Muḥibbī, 26
al-muhmal, 29–30
al-mujazzam, 29, 50, 52
al-mukhammas al-mardūd, 29, 180, 185
al-mūsijān, 27
al-nabr, 21, 145
al-nadb, 30, 50, 54, 58, 162–67
al qarīḍ, 27

al-qarrādī, 29, 30 n. 18, 33–39, 50, 53–54, 58–60, 79–84, 103–7, 109, 111–14, 116–20, 127, 144, 154–55, 157–58, 180, 185, 192, 194
al-qaṣīd, 28, 50, 52, 144. *See also qaṣīd*
al-qaṣīd al-badawī, 31, 50, 174
al-qūmā, 27
al-shammarī, 174
al-shiʿr al-lubnānī, 10
al-shiʿr al-qawmī, 10
al-shiʿr al-shaʿbī, 10
al-shiʿr al-ʿāmmī, 10, 35, 56
al-shurūqī, 31, 36, 50, 55, 57–58, 155, 170, 174–76, 179
al-Tikrītī, Anṭūn, 40
al-Yāzijī, al-Shaykh Nāṣīf, 54
al-zaghrada, 50
al-zaḥfa, 3
al-zalghaṭa, 30, 50, 54, 58, 167–70
al-zāmil, 3
ʿAql, Saʿīd, 1
ʿAr-rūzanā, 76
Assemanus, 152
ʿatābā, 30, 36, 50, 53–54, 58, 129–34, 137–43, 146, 149, 152, 179–80, 194
ʿAwwād, Tawfīq, 19 n. 23, 35–36, 38, 54, 144
awzān, 28, 41–42
ʿAytāt, 155
badīʿ, 29
balīq, 26
basīṭ, 34, 42–43, 54, 57–59, 69–70, 72, 74–75, 97, 154–56, 166, 170–73, 175, 177–78, 193
Bayrūtī, 126–27
bayt, 6 n. 4, 33 n. 31, 99 n. 157, 100–101, 129–31, 133, 136, 138–39, 141, 143, 146–47
Bedouin, 3, 31, 117, 174–75
Biqāʿī, 126–27
Cheikho, Louis, 133
counting rhymes, 79, 107, 114
Dalmann, Gustaf, 39
dalʿūnā, 36, 58–59, 76, 126–27
de Saussure, Ferdinand, 14
dīwān, 28, 156
Ephrem the Syrian, Saint, 37–38, 55, 103
Fayrouz, 187, 189–91
Frayḥa, Anīs, 10, 35, 36 n. 39
fuṣḥā, 9–10, 14–15, 17, 19–22, 26–28, 32–35, 43–45, 56, 60, 63, 65–72, 75–76, 79, 87, 92–95, 97, 100, 104, 106, 112 n. 15, 114, 132, 136–37, 138 n. 11, 142–43, 146, 148–49, 151–54, 164, 166, 170–71, 174–75, 179, 193–94
ghazal, 26, 119
ḥamāq, 26–27
ḥawraba, 30 n. 20, 165–66

hemistich, 18, 22 n. 27, 33, 42–48, 50–51, 54, 63–66, 68–70, 71 n. 12, 80, 85, 88–92, 94 n. 148, 99 n. 156, 105–7, 109–10, 112, 114, 117–19, 127, 129–32, 134, 136–43, 147–48, 150 n. 18, 151–52, 154, 156–57, 159–60, 162, 168–72, 179–80, 182–86, 188
ḥidā, 50, 53–54, 58–59, 109, 111, 154–58, 161, 166, 194
Hispano-Arabic, 5, 9, 125
huzām, 120–21
Iberian Peninsula, 5
ibn al-dhakā, 12
ibn al-fann, 12
ibn al-kār, 12
Ibn Khaldūn, 27, 39
Ibn Quzmān, 5
idiograms, 191
Imruʾ al-Qays, 14
Iraq, 3, 113
iṣābat al-maʿnā, 12–13, 79, 95
iʿlāl, 22, 63
Jalakh, Asʿad, 67
jalwet al-ʿarūs, 30
jannāz, 36
jawqa, 1–2, 16, 101 n. 160, 134 n. 8
Karshūnī, 35 n. 38, 106
kasrit mījanā, 130
Katz, Israel, 85 n. 142, 86, 162
khabab, 33–34, 39, 59–61, 157
kharja, 5 n. 3, 6 n. 4, 30 n. 18
khuzām, 120–22, 125
Kisirwān, 42, 120 n. 23
Kurpershoek, Marcel, 4
laḥn afrāmī, 103
Layyā w-layyā, 76, 116–17
Lebanon, 1, 3, 9 n. 1, 11 n. 11, 13 n. 15, 17 n. 21, 19, 29, 42, 45, 53, 56, 63, 65, 69, 79, 99 n. 156, 113, 120, 126 n. 27, 129, 135, 145, 155, 185, 187
Lecerf, Jean, 36–39, 106–7, 129–30, 144, 172–73
Littmann, Enno, 39
Mamlūks, 69
Maronite, 13, 35, 55, 103, 113, 152, 194
maṭlaʿ, 28, 30 n. 18, 36, 144, 173–74, 180–82, 184–90
mawāliyya, 27 n. 8
mawwāl, 36, 58, 179–81
mawzūn, 37
maʿannā, 10–11, 13 n. 15, 26, 28–29, 33, 35–36, 38, 41, 50, 52–54, 58–59, 66, 79–87, 89, 93, 95–101, 125, 134, 144–46, 148–49, 152, 155–56, 185, 194
maʿannā muwashshaḥ, 120
maʿṣūb, 136, 140
mījanā, 30, 36, 50, 53, 55, 58, 76, 129–35, 138–40, 149, 152, 171, 179–80, 194

mkhammas mardūd, 180
Muḥīṭ al-muḥīṭ, 32
mujazzam, 29, 50, 52
mukaffir, 26
mutadārik, 33
muthallathāt, 132–33
muwashshaḥa, 5–6, 9, 120, 121 n. 25, 125
muzaylij, 26
Nabati poetry, 3–4
nagham, 30–31
Nakhleh, Amīn, 11, 26, 28–32, 50, 103, 132, 144
Nakhleh, Rashīd, 26, 29, 50, 53, 156
naqā'id, 3
nathr al-naghamāt, 79, 84, 97, 129, 134, 138, 148–49, 168, 170, 175–76, 194
naẓm al-naghamāt, 30, 40–41, 79, 84, 126, 158, 162, 164, 170, 176, 180, 192, 194
Palestine, 3, 9 n. 1, 113
proto-tune, 86–90, 93, 99, 134, 139–40, 171, 176–77
qaṣīd, 31, 36, 52, 54, 59, 101, 144–52, 174, 185, 194. See also *al-qaṣīd*
qaṣīd maʿannā, 101
qawwāl, 11–12
Quṭrub, 132–33
rabāb, 174
raddet maʿannā, 100–101
rajaz, 17–18, 33, 35, 58–59, 66–69, 74–75, 87–89, 91–93, 95, 97–100, 129, 133, 140, 145–46, 149, 151–52, 154–56, 159, 166, 193
rawiyy, 29
riddādeh, 1–2, 194
rujūʿ, 29, 147–48
Sābā, Asʿad, 12
Salāma, Būlus, 63, 65
sarīʿ, 33, 35, 42–43, 50, 54, 58–59, 74–75, 144–46, 149, 151–52
Ṣaʿb, William, 12, 155
Seybold, Christian Friedrich, 32
Shamsiddin, Nasri, 187
shāʿir, 11–12
Shiʿite, 113
shrūqiyya, 174
Shūf district, 29, 155
shurūqī, 31, 36, 50, 55, 57–58, 155, 170, 174–76, 179
Shwayfāt, 155
Shʿayb, Zayn, 134
Sowayan, Abdullah, 4–5
Syria, 3, 9 n. 1, 110, 113
Syriac, 10, 35–37, 39–40, 55–56, 103–4, 106
Talḥūq, Sheikh Nāyef, 155
Ṭarafa ibn al-ʿAbd, 14
tatlīt, 133
Ṭrād, Michel, 12
Tripoli (Lebanon), 69–70
Vatican, 106

vernacular, 4–6, 9–12, 14, 16, 21–22, 26–28, 30–31, 35, 43, 56, 58, 63–67, 69, 72, 88 n. 144, 100, 109 n. 11, 112 n. 15, 133, 145–46, 152, 154, 169
Vilmar, Edvardus, 132
wāfir, 28–29, 33, 35, 58–59, 74–75, 97, 129, 136, 140, 142–46, 149, 151–53
waṣla, 15, 17
Weil, Gotthold, 76
Whaybeh, Munīr, 19 n. 23, 21 n. 25, 40–42, 44–57, 60, 132, 144, 165–66, 179
Ya-ghzayyil, 116, 118
Zaghlūl al-Dāmūr, 17 nn. 20–21, 48, 54, 99 n. 156, 101 n. 160, 125 n. 26, 131 nn. 2, 4, 134, 136 n. 10, 145, 156 n. 23, 159 n. 27, 176. *See also* al-Hāshim, Joseph
zajal, 1, 3–5, 7, 9–14, 16, 19–23, 25–33, 35–41, 43–44, 46–47, 48 n. 67, 49–50, 53–59, 63, 65, 67, 69–70, 72, 74–79, 85 n. 142, 89, 93, 95, 96 n. 151, 97–100, 101 n. 160, 120–21, 125, 131 n. 2, 133, 134 n. 8, 144–46, 152, 155–56, 162, 165–66, 174, 179–80, 183, 185–87, 193–95
zajjāl, 11–12, 16
Zaydān, Jurjī, 32, 35, 38
ziḥāf, 22, 66, 72, 98

About the Team

Geoffrey Khan and Alessandra Tosi were the managing editors for this book.

Krisztina Szilagyi performed the copyediting of the book in Word. The fonts used in this volume are Charis SIL and Scheherazade New.

Cameron Craig created all of the editions — paperback, hardback, and PDF. Conversion was performed with open source software freely available on our GitHub page at https://github.com/OpenBookPublishers.

Jeevanjot Kaur Nagpal designed the cover of this book. The cover was produced in InDesign using Fontin and Calibri fonts.

www.ingramcontent.com/pod-product-compliance
Lightning Source LLC
Chambersburg PA
CBHW050524170426
43201CB00013B/2075
* 9 7 8 1 8 0 5 1 1 3 9 1 1 *